# RAILW OF
# HELL

# RAILWAY OF HELL

by

## REGINALD BURTON

LUX VITAE

Burton

Pen & Sword
**MILITARY**

First published in 1963 by Macdonalds
under the title *The Road to Three Pagodas*

Republished in a revised and extended edition
in Great Britain in 2002 by
Leo Cooper

Reprinted in this format in 2010 by
Pen & Sword Military
*an imprint of*
Pen & Sword Books Ltd
47 Church Street
Barnsley
South Yorkshire S70 2AS

ISBN 978 1 84884 299 1

A CIP catalogue record for this book is
available from the British Library

Printed and bound in England
by CPI

*Pen & Sword Books Ltd incorporates the imprints of*
Pen & Sword Aviation, Pen & Sword Maritime, Pen & Sword Military,
Wharncliffe Local History, Pen & Sword Select,
Pen & Sword Military Classics and Leo Cooper,
Remember When, Seaforth Publishing and Frontline Publishing

*For a complete list of Pen & Sword titles please contact*
PEN & SWORD BOOKS LIMITED
47 Church Street, Barnsley, South Yorkshire, S70 2AS, England
E-mail: enquiries@pen-and-sword.co.uk
Website: www.pen-and-sword.co.uk

ARMA VIRUMQUE CANO

Virgil, *Aeneid*

To my fellow prisoners-of-war of all nationalities who suffered captivity in Malaya, Thailand and Burma. To the survivors, especially to my friend John Hayne, and to the memory of those who died, including Alan Woodbridge, my batman.

To the officers and men of the 4th Battalion, the Royal Norfolk Regiment, and in particular to those of D Compnay, this book is also dedicated.

# CONTENTS

# ACKNOWLEDGEMENTS

I am indebted to Ronald Searle for allowing his drawings to be re-produced in this book, and a brief note of explanation would be appropriate. During captivity, he somehow managed to conjure up drawing and colouring materials. His art and ingenuity made it possible to put on concert parties and shows, providing posters, programmes, sets and backdrops for the stage. His success on his return to civilian life is well deserved. I have still the originals which hang in pride of place on my study walls. I would also like to thank Professor Sears Eldredge of Macalester College, St Paul, U.S.A. for his gift of photos which he took while on a visit, after the war, to the Railway and the River Kwai. Finally I am grateful to Jane Flower, (the official Historian of Japanese Captivity) for all the help and advice she gave me in the preparation of my manuscripts.

# FOREWORD

When I originally wrote this book, which then appeared under the title *The Road to Three Pagodas*, I was a serving officer. I therefore had to submit my manuscript to the War Office for scrutiny and approval. Unfortunately, some of the grimmer aspects of Japanese brutality and atrocity had to be 'diluted' in the original edition. The Staff Officer who interviewed me explained that it was not advisable, in the prevailing spirit of reconciliation, that the book be published as I had written it, since under the circumstances it might be construed as official British Army policy. He mentioned the help that the Japanese had given us in the Korean War. He also mentioned the amount of trade we did with them and how important it was that this should not be adversely affected.

Nevertheless, now that I have retired, I am at liberty to present the truth as it unfolded, without any embellishment or constraint, hence this new edition. I was very grateful to Captain B. H. Liddell Hart for writing to me and giving me encouragement. He was one of our foremost military historians and his history of World War I is still required reading at Sandhurst.

I have made no criticism of the tactical and strategic handling, by Higher Command, of the Battle of Malaya culminating in the Fall of Singapore, except to try to alter the general belief that we outnumbered the Japanese. This may well have been the case on paper, but in terms of actual numbers engaged in fighting we were outnumbered.

When General Percival, our Commander-in-Chief, surrendered to General Yamashita, the Japanese Commander-in-Chief, the latter was completely amazed at the number of non-combatant troops handed over. As Singapore was General Headquarters Far East, there was an enormous establishment of Ancillary Troops, namely Administrative Units, which took no part in the actual fighting. The Japanese Army, by contrast, dispensed with the luxury of large medical supply and maintenance units, and was trained to live off the land and fend for itself.

It was not surprising that the Japanese, who glorified death in battle, were at a complete loss as to how to handle such large numbers of prisoners. This may have accounted in some measure for their contempt, and brutal handling, as it subsequently turned out. This, of course, is no excuse for their behaviour and their continual violation of International Law and the Geneva Convention. I know from my own experience that the British Infantry Regiments fought extremely well. My own D Company of the 4th Battalion The Royal Norfolk Regiment had, at the time of the surrender lost nearly all its officers: three platoon commanders, the company commander and the second-in-command of the company were all battle casualties.

It would seem that when the Japanese forced prisoners to sign forms saying that they would not escape, this culminated in the horrible Selerang Incident. Furthermore, their use of prisoners in war factories, especially for forced labour in building a railway through the dense Thai jungles to Burma to sustain their campaign there, must be always remembered. I feel it is my duty to record these matters faithfully in this new edition, to point out that the brutalization of men incapable of standing up for themselves is hardly in keeping with Bushido, the accepted Japanese code of honour. Those few who retaliated did so in certain knowledge of death by decapitation or torture.

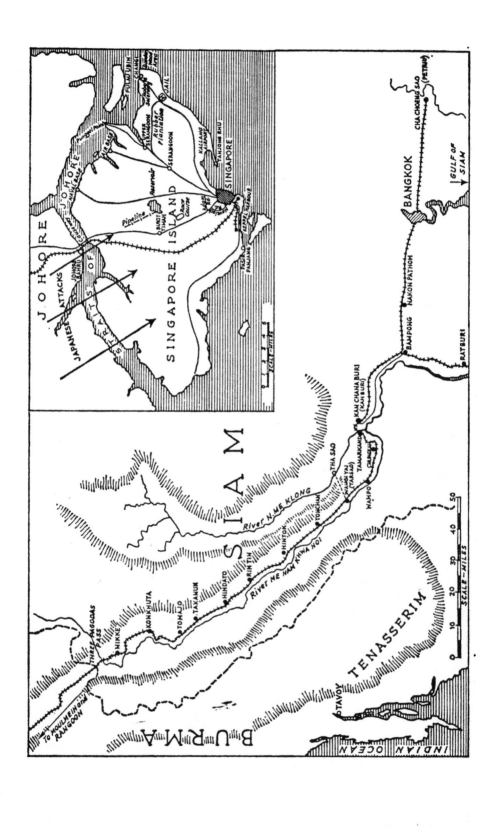

# Chapter 1

## THE OUTBREAK OF WORLD WAR II
## 1939–1941

At the outbreak of war in September 1939 I was a Junior Officer serving with my Regiment, the 1st Battalion The Royal Norfolk Regiment, in Bangalore, Southern India. Known as the Garden City of India, it was situated in Mysore State where the Maharajah was a beneficent autocrat, very loyal to the British Raj. The general atmosphere of the place was most congenial, as was the attitude of its people.

The war in Europe seemed a very long way off, and we read of the Fall of France and the Dunkirk Evacuation with a feeling of foreboding. At that time we were mostly engaged in Platoon, Company, and Battalion Training and exercises. As the British Battalion in the Mysore State we were primarily responsible for internal security and crowd control when necessary. This was put to the test whenever we were visited by the political dignitaries of the Indian Congress Party. They included such VIPs as Mahatma Gandhi, Nehru and Bose, to name but a few. It was a difficult time, as they were demanding Home Rule (Swah Raj), which we agreed must come eventually, but at the time it would have been impossible since we were in the shadow of a global war. This was brought home to most when Japan entered the conflict and subsequently arrived at the gateways to India.

Eventually the invasion of Britain became a very strong possibility. It was in the summer of 1940 that we, along with eight other Infantry Regiments, left India for England to bolster up the meagre resources. Although the miracle of Dunkirk had extricated most of our men we had lost all our heavy equipment, vehicles, artillery and armour.

Upon our arrival in England the Battalion was posted to the 20th

1

Independent Guards Brigade, consisting of ourselves, the 2nd Irish Guards and the 2nd Welsh Guards. Our job was to defend most of the outer boundary of South London in the area of Croydon, and the operation was code-named 'Brown Line'.

One evening in September 1940 I was Orderly Officer on duty when I received the code-word "CROMWELL" from Brigade Headquarters, which meant that invasion was imminent. We immediately rushed to our prepared positions and stood to for seventy-six hours. Apparently, as we were to learn afterwards, the Germans were rehearsing for the invasion in barges in the Calais area and the RAF had rather hindered their exercises.

At the end of 1940 I was told that I had been ordered to leave the 1st Battalion and moved to the 4th Battalion which was part of 54 Brigade in the 18th Infantry Division (Territorial Army). They had been in defence positions on the Norfolk coast, but were now stationed in Scotland where I proceeded with due haste. At this time it was generally thought that the invasion scare had died down for the time being.

Before going overseas the Division was moved to Lancashire, where we were engaged in a large-scale manoeuvre against the 2nd Division, who were stationed in Yorkshire. This was appropriately code-named 'The War of the Roses'. The 2nd Division had recently returned from Dunkirk, where they had put up a gallant action, fighting in the rearguard of the British Expeditionary Force. This rearguard action had engaged the 2nd Battalion The Royal Norfolk Regiment which gained several decorations, awarded on the beaches of Dunkirk; one in particular was that of Company Sergeant Major Gristock, who was awarded a posthumous VC. The Regiment won five VCs during the war, the most won by a single British Infantry Regiment. Before arriving on the Dunkirk beaches the Battalion had seen many engagements. One of these, at a village called Le Paradis, resulted in one Company having to surrender. It was then massacred by the Germans, instead of being taken prisoner. On arrival in Yorkshire the surviving men were very much depleted, and were re-grouping and re-training. Thus it was not surprising that the 18th Division won the battle, and were consequently earmarked for overseas service instead of the 2nd Division, who were later on destined for Burma where they put up a magnificent defence at Kohima, which was as far as the Japanese reached in their invasion of India.

It is interesting to note that had the 2nd Division won the exercise they would have finished up in Malaya and the 18th Division would have gone to Burma: so much for the hinge of fate.

It was not until October 1941 that, after embarkation leave, we proceeded to Liverpool and embarked on the SS *Andes*, to join a large convoy assembling in the Irish Sea.

And so we went to war.

# Chapter 2

## OUTWARD BOUND

## 1941–1942

We sailed at lunchtime and in the afternoon we had joined a convoy in the Irish Sea with the remainder of the ships of the Division which had embarked in Glasgow. We were very amused at the escort which happened to be of four old Destroyers, (with their pencil-shaped funnels). They were part of an exchange deal with the Americans for bases in the West Indies.

The first few days out were extremely rough, and nearly all the troops were laid low with seasickness. At noon on the third day, when most people were recovering up on deck, we met the most enormous convoy of merchantmen we had ever seen; the ships literally covered the entire horizon. Our old Destroyers left us at this point, and we found that our new escort (departing from the enormous merchant convoy) was entirely American. A Battleship (*New Mexico* Class), an Aircraft Carrier (*Saratoga* Class), four Cruisers and eight Destroyers. This was a part of the lend-lease agreement between Churchill and Roosevelt, for as yet the USA were not in the war.

At this time our fortunes were at their lowest and most dangerous period in the Battle of the Atlantic. The American help then was a much needed godsend.

After about six days steaming from Liverpool we eventually reached Halifax. We were surprised to see waiting in the harbour three of the largest liners in the world, namely the *America* (renamed USS *West Point*), *Manhattan* (renamed the USS *Wakefield*) and the *Washington* (renamed the USS *Mount Vernon*).

It was night-time when our ship the *Andes* came alongside the

4

jetty. The troops had spent the evening looking at the lights of Halifax, blazing away without a blackout or any restrictions apparent to us. I was particularly fascinated to stare at all the lights and silhouettes of a great port in wartime, with all the ships bustling with activity. As I was detailed for a fatigue party unloading weapons and stores it was after midnight when I eventually arrived on board the *Wakefield*. I dumped my kit with four other officers in a cabin, which we were told had been used by Paulette Goddard in happier days.

As I was late on board I missed supper, but a friendly American Duty Officer took me down to the Officers' Mess, where an enormous negro steward regaled me with ham and eggs and black coffee, and all sorts of questions about England and the House of Lords. This giant of a man had a great sense of humour and was to become a great favourite with the British Officers.

Our voyage down the American coast began at dawn. The three large transports contained the three Infantry Brigades of the Division, whilst the Ancillary units travelled in smaller vessels. The escort had been reduced to the Aircraft Carrier, two cruisers and four destroyers.

We eventually arrived in Trinidad where we were told there was to be no shore leave. Fortunately I had found out that my Uncle Rupert Burton R.N. was commanding the Naval Air Base at Piarco. My cousin Bill and I were allowed ashore and were met by a Naval Staff car and taken out to the base. There we spent a very pleasant day having lunch and tea and being shown round. Eventually we had to return to the ship and we were back on board in good time to sail that evening.

From now on our escort consisted of the two Cruisers and the four Destroyers. This was to be one of the longest parts of the voyage and it was approximately ten days before we reached Cape Town.

During this part of the voyage we crossed the line and our American hosts went to great pains to entertain us with the arrival on board of King Neptune and his merry court. The fun was fast and furious and when it looked like getting out of hand the Captain sounded the alarm, 'General Quarters'. As we went to our action stations we were all convinced an attack had been spotted, whether by surface raider or submarine, but it appeared later after the stand down that it had only been a quick and effective way of restoring law and order!

During the last part of this long leg of our voyage we went very far south of Cape Aguilhas to enter Cape Town from the eastern approach. During the night we ran into the worst storm I have ever known at sea – our cabin furniture was literally hurled all over the place. It was funny lying in the top bunk, hanging on like hell, to watch all the drawers sliding in and out of the chest of drawers and to see the unlatched cabin door swinging open and shut. The camp bed in the middle of the cabin slid backwards and forwards nearly all night. Whether the occupant really slept or not I shall never know!

Eventually we reached Cape Town and it was at this point that the attack on Pearl Harbor was given out on the ship's radio. I remember thinking at the time that, no matter what happened now, we could not possibly lose the war. We were granted shore leave and the people of Cape Town turned out in their hundreds to meet us and to offer us the hospitality of their homes. I feel sure their kindness and generosity will always be remembered and at that time in particular they gave us a series of happy memories to brighten the dark and perilous days that lay ahead.

We sailed on through the Indian Ocean and spent Christmas Day at sea. We had a very good Christmas dinner consisting chiefly of Maryland chicken and other American delicacies. We eventually reached Bombay after 53 Brigade had been dispatched to Mombasa in the USS *Mount Vernon* and so routed on directly to Singapore. We, the remainder of the Division, arrived in Bombay and entrained for Ahmednagar, where we stayed about a fortnight, spent mostly in training. One day we were paraded and told we were returning to Bombay. We embarked on the very same transports and in exactly the same cabins we had so recently vacated, little thinking that we would ever see them again or at the most so soon afterwards. We sailed on, thinking by this time that our voyage might never come to an end.

As usual there was speculation about our final destination. After 53 Brigade had left us off the East Coast of Africa rumour had been rife: we had thought they had gone on to the Middle East while we went to India. In point of fact, we learned later that they had been thrown piece-meal into the battle on the Malayan mainland.

Eventually we rounded Ceylon and proceeded in an easterly direction. At this point we could guess our destination with certainty.

I shall always remember the last few days of our long sea journey, which had taken us nearly half round the world and touched on four of the five continents. We passed through the Sunda Straits and saw Krakotoa on the horizon. It resembled an enormous shark's fin, blue and hazy in the tropical shimmer. As we turned north and wended our way through the Banka Straits the ships took up a position of single file or line astern. I was on the top deck at the time, looking back at the graceful lines of the USS *West Point* (the *America*) when suddenly I saw what I thought was a tropical waterspout on one side of her and then another nearer and then another on the far side. It was such a beautiful day my mind was not connected with the horror of war. Then suddenly every ack-ack gun in the convoy opened with a crashing crescendo. I looked up and saw our Japanese enemies, almost invisible so high were they in the sky, indulging in what we eventually learned to call 'pattern bombing'. Fortunately no ships were hit, and that night we raced through the darkness with every bolt in the ship quivering with the extra speed.

The two big ships, our own *Wakefield* and the *West Point*, by keeping up a high speed, had pulled ahead of the convoy and early the next morning they moved smoothly into Keppel Harbour, Singapore. We'd expected to see a blitzed city, with ruined buildings and the black smoke of unquenched fires, but the first impression was one of absolute peace. The rich green of the many islets with their palms and dense vegetation were a reminder that we were in the tropics, but the waterfront buildings of Singapore were Western.

It was only as we docked that we saw things were not as usual. The jetties and quays were deserted. Everywhere there were bomb craters. The harbour installations had suffered badly and many a crane slanted drunkenly towards the water. I had expected, in spite of war, all the bustle and excitement of another Bombay, the dockside to be swarming with shouting and gesticulating coolies and so forth. None appeared.

There was a brooding tenseness which was depressing, killing the normal excitement of a journey's end. The troops were rather subdued.

There were other ships in the harbour and all seemed to be embarking civilian men, women and children. There were sailors – survivors from the HMS *Repulse* or HMS *Prince of Wales*, which had been sunk a week before by Japanese aircraft. And there were airmen, too. It was puzzling, a little disturbing. If we were hoping to hold Singapore, why were so many Service personnel leaving?

This sight certainly didn't do anything to boost the spirits of our men. One or two looked at me, as though inquiringly. I was glad there were no questions. I'd plenty of my own. Why weren't the Japs stopping us? The scenes around showed they had plenty of experience of bombing the harbour. What better target, then, than a division of troops landing?

We had snatched breakfast at first light, and as soon as we came alongside we were hurried ashore. There wasn't much in the way of a reception, but John remarked that somebody must have realized we'd arrived because there were open trucks waiting, with irrepressibly cheerful Australian drivers. I herded some twenty of my men into the back of one and then climbed into the cab beside the driver, who at once informed me that he'd driven all down the peninsula, chased by the "Nip bastards". But he was full of optimism. "We'll come good on the island," he said, giving the last word the full treatment of Australian accent and almost making it unrecognizable.

As we moved off an air raid started. I wondered if it was the big one I'd been anticipating all night. We'd left a baggage party to help with unloading. I hoped they'd be all right. Then my hopes were transferred to my own survival and that of the men in the open back of the truck. They'd only kit bags for seats and several had been forced to stand.

Our driver seemed out to break records. I could well understand why the "Nip bastards" had never caught up with him during the flight down the long peninsula. He chattered away, quite unconcerned, while he took bends in the manner of a movie stunt man!

I managed to get a few glimpses of the city, which was just awakening to the toil and cares of the day. Some of the streets were very European in appearance, others were definitely oriental. There was, to me, the fascinating clatter of Chinese clogs on the pavements as the crowds filled the streets. The street vendors were active, crying their wares. The sellers of ice-cream clacked bits of wood together musically. There was little to suggest war. At one point a party of attractive European women in summery dresses crossed the road, dodging our recklessly driven truck. I waved to them and they waved back and smiled. I was given a false reassurance, thinking that as they were still here the situation couldn't be as grave as I'd feared.

But soon enough there was a grim reminder of war. We sped on past a large airport which the Australian told me was Kallang. I could see the runways were cratered. Buildings and hangars were damaged, but most depressing of all were the large burnt-out craters. These must have contained desperately-needed fighters and my apprehension returned since I knew that without air support we'd be at a crushing disadvantage.

The drive became less hazardous because we were virtually clear of traffic and speeding along the east coast road.

After a time I saw a large white building on our right, "What's that?" I asked.

"Changi Jile," was the immediate reply. It took me a moment or so to grasp his pronunciation of 'jail'. Fortunately for my peace of mind at the time I was blissfully ignorant of how familiar this place was to become.

We turned away from the coast and at last reached our destination. It was a rubber plantation. Camouflaged tents had already been erected among the trees, which were planted so uniformly that they formed straight avenues in all directions. The effect was rather monotonous, though the sun-dappled shade was pleasant and the cover gave a feeling of security. We pulled up and the troops clambered out stiffly. They looked a bit dazed. Among them was my batman Alan Woodbridge. He was a burly figure and there was a twinkle in his eye as he asked me, "Did we break the world's speed record, Sir?"

This camp was for C and D Companies. The rest of the battalion was farther down the road. I was soon joined by John, then Percy and Lazenby Jones (Jonah). They, as platoon commanders, had their respective platoons with them. As second-in-command of D Company I'd arrived first to attend to administrative details. They gathered around and it was clear from their comments that their ride out had been every bit as hair-raising as my own.

Finally Tom Phillips, D Company commander, pulled up. He'd stayed to see all the men off the ship.

"I feel like putting my driver on a charge," he grumbled. "You can't do that to a fellow cobber," I said. I wondered if these Australians always drove in a reckless manner, or whether they'd had special instructions to get us away from the docks and to our positions as quickly as possible. If so, they'd carried out their orders to the letter.

We lost no time in unpacking and settling in. Just as we were doing this we had our first visitor. He was a Tamil with copies of the local Singapore papers, which he quickly sold out. He was on to us so promptly I felt he must have been waiting for us to arrive.

9

The news columns of the papers did nothing to cheer us. The Japanese were advancing. Unfamiliar with most of the place names, we could only guess at what progress the enemy had made. John said, "You can bet the actual situation's worse than anything written here. There's sure to be some sort of security delay in releasing the bad news."

I felt that uncertainty was worse than full knowledge could ever have been. We'd simply no idea how far we were from the advance units of the Japanese army. Later in the day our Commanding Officer, Lt.-Col. Knights, arrived. He was a small, wiry man and, whatever his real feelings, he always managed to persuade us that things could be much worse. He hadn't a great deal of information to offer, but he advised us not to unpack more than was necessary. We might be moved to the coastline in the morning. He said that the men we'd left behind unloading the *Wakefield* had been caught in the air raid, but he didn't know if there had been any casualties. We rested, looking through the newspapers again, concentrating on the adverts for Tiger Beer and other more attractive commodities. They provided an escape.

Darkness came. I didn't turn in immediately. There were the strange night sounds of the insects and other nocturnal creatures.

And now the long voyage was over and I was outside a tent in a rubber plantation on Singapore Island, wondering what was to happen to me next.

Looking back, I see this night as a turning point in my life. I couldn't foresee the future. I knew, of course, that it was filled with danger and that the prospects were grim. I didn't believe, though, that there could be an absolute disaster. A long and bitter siege, yes. This was probably going to be something like England during that perilous and testing summer of 1940. But England had survived ruthless assault. Surely we could do the same thing in Singapore?

I knew that almost overnight I should reach a maturity and become hardened and experienced, and that my entire life would be changed beyond recognition. But the warning voices were sounding. Not merely the distant artillery fire. There was action much nearer. I listened and knew it must be an air raid. Were the docks catching it again? Were some of our men still there? Would the *Wakefield* survive and get clear?

There were no immediate answers to these questions. Suddenly around me everything seemed very still. We might have been quartered in a vast cathedral, for the orderly rows of the rubber trees were like great columns, and the moss underfoot was a soft carpet.

I was worried and anxious, but I was also very tired. I turned in and the artillery fire and bomb-dropping resumed in the distance. Eventually I fell asleep.

# Chapter 3

## INTO BATTLE

## 1942

Our stay in the comparative quietness of the rubber plantation was brief. It was a strange experience because we knew little of what was happening and this, helped by our surroundings, gave us a feeling of being isolated from it all. This was increased by the fact that we had been detached from the rest of the battalion, and when we moved it was to be in support of another battalion, but in the same brigade.

There were constant reminders of the struggle in progress. We could hear the artillery fire and the air raids; but we'd little information about how the fighting was going, or indeed where exactly it was taking place. The grimmer humorists forecast that we'd know soon enough; it would be our turn next; but there was an alternative suggestion that we'd been sent to the wrong place and would be left here for the duration, nobody at H.Q. knowing what had become of us.

In our ignorance there was no thought, either among officers or men, that we were facing defeat. We realized it wasn't going to be a picnic. We were in for a long and testing siege, with some tough fighting whenever the Japs tried to cross from Johore. But we'd hold out and build up for the time when we could go over to the attack.

"We always get off to a poor start," John summed it up.

Our discussions on the future of the campaign were interrupted by orders to move into position on the north-east corner of Singapore Island. The entire northern coastline is separated from the Malayan peninsula by a strait which is approximately a quarter of a mile wide. It was quite clear we were going to take part in the defence of a coastal sector.

It was on a Sunday afternoon, in heavy tropic rainfall, that we marched into Upper Serangoon village. This was mainly inhabited by Chinese, and their box-like, open-fronted shops lined the road on both sides. Actually this was one end of a long, straggling village which started in Serangoon and finally petered out at a jetty in Serangoon Creek. Around the creek were a few Malay houses, occupied by land workers or fishermen. In contrast with the somewhat primitive homes there was a quite splendid church and a large monastery alongside it.

There was a contrast of another kind. As we marched in, ready for battle, a service had just finished and the villagers – most of whom seemed to be Christian – were just coming from the church. Was it just another Sunday to them? Did they realize what was happening?

Our C and D Companies of the 4th Royal Norfolk Regiment were placed under command of Major John Packard, the battalion second-in-command. This arrangement was advisable because we were rather remote from the rest of the battalion, and it emphasized that we were detached and had become an almost separate entity. We were in reserve to the 5th Suffolks, who were holding Punggol Point.

Serangoon Creek itself was a dividing line. The eastern side was held by the 4th Suffolks and they had in support the rest of our battalion under the C.O., Lt.-Col. Knights.

Our march ended in the village. We were to be billeted around the church. The men were in a hutment normally used by the local Boy Scouts. The officers were across the road in the monastery. Our host was an elderly French monk, a delightful chap. When we moved on we left our tin trunks and heavy luggage in his care. In September 1945 I was able to return to this monastery only to find it deserted. I learnt that the old monk had died. The Japs had pillaged the church and the monastery and our possessions were among the loot.

For me the stay in Upper Serangoon was short. One of our duties was to do wiring and carry out patrol activity for the 5th Suffolks and be in reserve to them. To perform their allotted tasks D Company moved halfway up the road leading to Punggol Point. I went with them and I very quickly assumed the responsibilities of the Command of the Company. I was in fact second-in-command, but the company commander developed a virulent attack of what was known as "Singapore Foot". This was a form of foot-rot due to sweat. He had to stay at the monastery.

Once more we found ourselves on a rubber plantation. This was

13

in a hollow and safe enough, comparatively speaking. But going on up the road the ground fell away to Punggol Point. This meant that the whole of the 5th Suffolks' position was exposed to observation from the thickly jungled Johore mainland. As soon as one reached the crest of the road there was a war-ravaged scene. There were the splintered remains of trees, and the ground was cratered nearly all the way down to the low mangroves which marked the swamps on the water's edge.

We shared our camp-site with an R.A.F. Repair and Maintenance Unit. Their C.O. was very helpful to us, but I was a little disconcerted when he said to me, "In confidence, I don't expect we'll be hanging on here much longer – we're awaiting evacuation to Java."

In similar confidence I passed on this information to the three officers who were my platoon commanders, Percy, John and Jonah. Jonah was a very solid, thick-set fellow, most reliable. He rarely said much, but when he did it was always to the point. He looked particularly grave at my news, and finally announced that he didn't like it.

"It can't be," John ventured, "that we're pulling out?"

It seemed unthinkable, but we were uneasy. It had been a shock to me when I'd first surveyed the point to realize that no defences had been put up. That there were no land mines was understandable. The humid climate virtually breeds corrosion. It would be very difficult to assess the 'life' of a minefield, and simply suicidal to judge the mines 'dead' and proceed to take them up. But there had been weeks during which barbed wire might have been put up. There wasn't any. Similarly there were no fortifications and no prepared positions.

We kept our far-from-cheerful thoughts from the troops. I felt the lack of information was having a bad effect on them, but we knew so little that there was really nothing we could do to remedy this situation. My training and my personal belief was that men will give more of themselves if told the exact position, however grim it may be. But I hadn't the vaguest idea of what was happening away from our sector. I couldn't achieve anything useful by passing on vague, unhappy doubts. I certainly couldn't have guessed that our division had been broken up into groups which were helping to man the perimeter of the island and that there was no reserve force in the centre available for emergency reinforcing.

Our first task was to put up barbed wire in front of the position held by the 5th Suffolks. Owing to the exposed nature of the country this would have to be done by night with the great disadvantage that no detailed daylight reconnaissance was possible. There was the risk, too, that once beyond our front line we might blunder into a Jap patrol probing across the straits.

I'd already decided that I should take part in the night excursions; by doing this we could work to a roster of one night out, one night in. We had the C.S.M. and the platoon sergeants helping, but I excluded the quartermaster-sergeant. He was having a harassing time because, with his staff, it was necessary to prepare daytime meals and also lay on food for the night parties. It was necessary for them to have a meal before setting out and they badly needed a breakfast when they returned at dawn.

Bearing in mind Napoleon's dictum about an army marching on its stomach, I was prepared to do everything possible to prevent the men who supplied the food from becoming involved in the fighting.

We were not left completely undisturbed. There was a baptism of fire when shells fell into D Company area, but fortunately it didn't develop into a systematic bombardment.

I disliked the wiring party work intensely. I'd found, during training at Aldershot, that it was extremely difficult to lay three-apron strand fences on firm ground in broad daylight. At Punggol Point we had to perform this in darkness, moving over swampy and unknown ground. We could only talk in whispers. Shells whistled over us, a reminder that there was an active enemy very near. But more than an encounter with the Japs I feared snakes. Sloshing around in the ooze I thought of water-snakes, cobras and kraits. It was sheer mental agony.

There was physical agony, too. We never seemed to have enough chain gloves – for hand protection. According to the wiring manual the wire should be grasped firmly in both hands between the barbs. This sounds simple enough, but in pitch darkness and with every possibility of someone bumping into me at the vital moment I invariably impaled my hands.

The need for silence seemed to increase the pain.

One dawn, returning from a wearying night of wiring, we experienced a hair-raising incident. We'd come through our lines and were actually on the road when we heard a pounding and saw a zebra charging straight at us. I was with the sergeant-major and we took to our heels. We knew we'd no chance against the obviously angry animal so long as we were in the open, so we rushed for the trees. It pursued us and we dodged this way and that. The sergeant-major wanted to shoot the beast in self-defence, but I was reluctant about this and dissuaded him. Eventually we reached our truck, which was sheltered from enemy view just below the ridge. I was far more terrified of the zebra than of being seen by the enemy.

The explanation of this extraordinary encounter was that there had been a zoo at Punggol Point. It had been shelled and there was nobody to care for the animals, so when the 5th Suffolks took up their position they released what animals they found there, at least giving them a chance of survival.

The idea that there were monkeys wandering around naturally inspired humorists among the men to utter warning against mistaking them for Jap intruders. There was also a slanderous story that Jonah had encountered a gorilla in the failing light and started to give it orders, mistaking it for his platoon sergeant.

It was good to have these lighter moments and I'm sure that the story of the encounter with the zebra gained quite a lot as it circulated among the men. My batman got hold of it and said how amusing it would be to be evacuated as a battle casualty, only to be told at the base hospital that one's wounds were the result of being bitten in action on the backside by an angry zebra.

When going through the 5th Suffolk lines on our wiring parties it was necessary to maintain close liaison, and here business was mixed with pleasure. Their forward company commander had a substantial dug-out in which there was a supply of whisky. I always felt there was a tinge of *Journey's End* about this setting; it seemed to belong more to the Somme than to Singapore, as we sat by the light of a candle in a bottle, swigging from another bottle and listening to the artillery fire going overhead in both directions.

Our other night activity brought us right back to the realities of the situation. Across the strait, just off our sector, there was an island called Pulau Ubin. It was long and narrow, and most of it was covered by rubber trees. These blended with the jungle background of Johore and it was very difficult from Serangoon to pick out the shape of the island even with the help of glasses.

It was believed that the island, which was much nearer the mainland than it was to us, had been occupied by the Japs, probably as a forward observation point. The brigadier wanted confirmation of this, and if the Japs were there he hoped for a prisoner. So we were warned to lay on patrols.

16

We were given a naval launch for the crossing and the first patrol was led by Percy. He had ten men with him. He and his party were taken by truck to the jetty in the creek. They boarded the launch and crossed without incident. The one good feature about Pulau Ubin was that it had a beach where one could jump out on to shingle and sand. Most of the coastline on both sides of the strait was mangrove swamp with thick black mud of varying depth. In some places one could struggle through the ooze, but others were as dangerous as any quicksands.

Just above the beach on Pulau Ubin there were a few Malay huts. These had been occupied by rubber tappers and their families, but Percy found them deserted. There was not much undergrowth on the island, just the groups of rubber trees, and he admitted that it was a rather nerve-racking business making their way through the lanes between the tree trunks apprehensive that Japs might appear from any direction.

Percy led his patrol to the solitary high point in the middle of the island. There were no Japs, but there was evidence they had been there. Raffia mats were laid out in a circle, and there were rifles, helmets, and equipment. He brought back samples of everything.

Why had the Japs left these things? It was a puzzle to which no one had a satisfactory answer. In the light of subsequent events I think it may have been part of a plan to deceive us into expecting an attack on our sector. Our patrol was anticipated. From the Johore jungle we often heard the clatter of mechanized vehicles, probably light tanks. Again, these may have kept up a regular patrol in order to give us the false impression that more and more material was arriving for the assault.

We were to make a second night patrol to Pulau Ubin, and this one I accompanied, though the actual patrol was under John Hayne's command.

As we were to set out at midnight it was necessary to snatch some sleep. We turned in after tea, but I know I didn't manage to drop off. I kept wondering about the circle of raffia mats. Had the Japs returned to the island and checked that we'd paid it a visit? And if so, was an ambush prepared for our return venture?

In retrospect I can't think why I did go on this patrol. There was plenty of other work for me as acting company commander and it was somewhat wasteful to make use of two officers when one would be sufficient. I was probably told to go for the experience, because it might easily have turned out to be my first close encounter with the enemy. I certainly don't remember volunteering for it.

We were roused at ten-thirty and a hot meal had been prepared. I don't think either John or I did it justice. When this was over, the patrol party fell in and checked equipment and weapons. There was one bright feature; we were travelling much lighter than when out on a wiring party. We were lightly clad and had only bare necessities. There was an unpleasant finality, though, about handing over all our personal possessions, emptying our pockets of all letters and photographs. There was to be nothing by which our unit could be identified in the event of our capture or death. I entrusted my belongings to Alan, my faithful batman, including my diary, telling him to look after it and drawing his attention to the phone numbers in it in the event of my not returning.

Then we climbed into the truck and were driven down to the jetty which marked the end of the Serangoon road. The Navy were waiting for us. We boarded the launch and sailed out of the creek and across the strait to the island. As the last man jumped ashore on the shingle, the launch slid away into the darkness. The arrangement was that it would return for us shortly before dawn.

We were on our own. At least I prayed we were. For all we knew the island might be crawling with Japs gleefully awaiting us. The natural instinct was to dive for cover and stay there until it was possible to make a dash for the launch.

We moved cautiously up the beach to the kampong, which was like a village of the dead. Here I was to establish the firm base while John pushed on to the high ground. The worst part of the business was waiting for him and his party to return. There was the eeriness of the deserted huts and there was a strange stillness; not exactly a silence, because the insects kept up a continuous shrilling. Now and then some bird with a fiendish cry would send a chill up my spine. Several times a toc-toc bird startled me, but at last I found him amusing and it cheered me up. In the distance there was the constant rumble of artillery fire. This was to the west and it seemed to me it was growing in intensity. This was the Japanese bombardment as a prelude to their invasion of the north-west corner of Singapore Island. I was told afterwards that while I was waiting on Pulau Ubin there was a reddish glow in the sky just over the dock area. This was from the oil tanks on Pulau Bukum.

At long last my vigil ended. John had reached the high ground

18

without incident. There were no raffia mats, he reported, and nothing in the way of equipment.

"Not a trace of a Jap," he said.

As we made our way down to the beach-head the end of the patrol was marred by tragedy. There was a mistake in recognition and fire was opened on the last men as they approached the beach. It was one of those mishaps which can happen so easily in the darkness and when nerves are tense.

The launch arrived and we boarded in shocked silence, carrying our casualties. One man died before we reached the security of Serangoon Creek.

"I never want to patrol that blasted island again," John muttered. We didn't.

The next morning a dispatch rider on a motor-bike roared into our camp. I was awakened to receive disturbing news and fresh orders. The Japanese had landed successfully in the north-west corner of the island, driving back the Australian defenders. They'd also repaired the Johore causeway and were crossing it. This causeway was very solidly built and was seventy feet wide at the water line. A gap had been blown by demolition charges, but it seemed that this could be negotiated at low tide and the Japs had managed some temporary repairs.

Our orders were to pull out immediately with C Company, rejoin the rest of the battalion and proceed to a position in the Bukit Timah area. This was a little to the north-west of Singapore itself and on the main road to the causeway.

The men seemed heartened by the prospect of going into battle. The gloom over the tragic ending of the previous night's patrol was swept away. I think, too, there was relief at the thought of no more night-time wiring parties. And for the battalion to be brought together put an end to a feeling of rather being out on our own.

I have to confess I was less cheerful. The previous night's patrol episode had shown up deficiencies of training, understandable after so long at sea, but serious on the eve of battle. More depressing was the news. We'd been so sure that we could hold the beaches – though swamps would be a more accurate description. How had the Japs managed to get across and drive back the seasoned and experienced Australian troops? What was going wrong? The news was so sketchy that it wasn't possible to visualize the tactical position.

It wasn't a time for thought, though. We were frantically busy getting our equipment together. Transport arrived – the same open trucks which had brought us from the docks to the rubber plantation – only this time the cheerful Australian drivers had been replaced by our own R.A.S.C. men.

"I expect we're more likely to reach our destination without being tipped out on the road with broken bones," John said, "but I rather miss those mad Australians."

I wondered why the change had been made, but it was yet another of the unanswered questions.

We linked up with C Company and we were delighted to see our company commander. He was hobbling around in gym shoes, supported by a long thumbstick. Unlike the rest of us he was wearing a peaked cap instead of a steel helmet.

John's forecast of a smoother ride wasn't borne out. The R.A.S.C. men drove as furiously as the Australians had. We went across country until we reached the Bukit Timah Road. It was a double carriageway, and there was the fantastic sight of an unending column of refugees making their way to Singapore. There were bullock carts, rickshaws, lorries, trishaws, bicycles, in fact everything available on wheels. Many were walking, loaded with shapeless baggage.

At one point, when our northern progress was slowed down, an oncoming lorry crowded with animated Chinese pulled up alongside my truck. Placards written in bold Chinese characters festooned the lorry and I'd no idea what they said, but the shouts and the attitudes of these men were certainly unfriendly. I had the impression they were demanding arms, or at least protection from the oncoming Japanese.

I'm sure that to the majority of the troops, whose normal horizons were bounded by King's Lynn in the north and Southend in the south, all these refugees looked alike. I remember thinking, rather vainly, that some lectures on Oriental physiognomy while aboard ship would have been a help. Perhaps reasons of security would have ruled them out. Looking at the refugee crowd of Chinese, Malays, Tamils and others, I wondered how many Japs had infiltrated and were spying out the disposition of our forces and defence points.

On the outskirts of Bukit Timah village we pulled up. We were just behind the racecourse, and here we dug in for the night. I was beginning to feel exhausted. I'd been up all the previous night because of going out with the patrol and I'd snatched only very little sleep the day before. The company commander limped up and told me to go to sleep in my weapon pit. I didn't need urging. I slept soundly, though I did have at the end of it one of the most vivid dreams of my life. I was back in Torquay, at Larchmont House, my prep school. It was a Saturday in summer and I was being taken out to tea by my dear mother, and then we went on the beach.

I awakened, cramped, and for a few seconds found it hard to accept the idea that I was involved in war – far too closely involved for comfort.

Our defensive position was a good one. We were on a gentle slope sparsely covered with a few trees and bushes. We overlooked a small valley which was rather overgrown with what appeared to be banana trees. There was some sort of a building but too hidden for us to identify it.

There'd been wiring work, but nothing like the ordeal of the night-time wiring parties at Punggol Point. And with dawn we stood to in our deep slit trenches. Suddenly there was an alarm. There was movement of some sort on our front; but we held our fire for the moment. We could hear voices.

"Urdu," I said to Tom Phillips. "Just as well we didn't open up."

"It could be a Jap trick," he said cautiously. "They call out in Urdu and pretend to be Gurkhas."

Percy and an N.C.O. went forward cautiously, to return laughing. In the small valley beneath us there was an Indian field bakery, blissfully ignorant that it was between our front line and the advancing Japanese. On being told they broke all records in packing up and disappearing from the scene. Needless to say, the discarded buckshee loaves soon found their way into the troops' haversacks.

There was, however, a graver side to this incident. How typical was it of the lack of information? We ourselves knew very little of what was going on beyond our particular sector. There was intensive artillery fire which seemed to come from all directions. The nature of the land, particularly with so many rubber plantations, made direct observation so limited as to be almost useless.

The morning drifted past and nothing happened. Then orders came through that we were to move out from our present positions, cross the racecourse and follow the pipe-line until we encountered Japanese advance units. We were to drive them back and throw them off the island.

It was an order which surprised me. Looking back, I still think we should have done much better had we been left in our prepared position. However, the order was clear enough. We started to advance in open formation. The incongruous seemed to be the rule. We reached the edge of a beautifully kept racecourse and marched down the straight towards the grandstand and enclosures. As we passed the tarmac entrances to the stand we saw they were stacked with crates of tinned food. These were in the open and many had been looted. It was the first indication of the state of anarchy which was soon to be all too familiar.

Once away from the racecourse we opened out again, moving in the cover of a hedge. We came to a clearing which contained a large pipe-line. This sloped away uphill to a cluster of trees on the skyline. It was from this direction that we could hear sporadic bursts of firing. I realized that at last we'd come to grips with the enemy.

We had A Company ahead of us. B Company with C in reserve was on our left. The 4th Suffolks were over on our right.

The firing increased, but as yet there was nothing coming at us. We started to climb the hill and very quickly we ran into the wounded from A Company making their way painfully back. They had evidently been taken by surprise and the casualties were severe. Uniforms were splashed with blood. Some men were limping, others were being helped along by less severely wounded comrades.

For a moment our own men wavered. They had friends, even relations, among the wounded, and their immediate reaction was to lend a hand. This was their first real experience of action and they had not had time to develop the necessary hardness which would enable them to concentrate on their own task. However, we quickly managed to get them on the move and as we neared the crest the momentum of our advance increased. But on the crest it was checked by very strong, close-range bursts of fire. We dived to the ground and crawled for cover.

Overhead there was the roar of aircraft. I looked up at the approaching Jap bombers. They were flying so low that I could see the pilots looking down. I saw, too, the bomb bays open and the bombs come slanting out. They slanted away from me, fortunately, but as I buried my head against the soil I could feel the ground shake like an enormous jelly. It had the same unsteadying effect as the 'cake walk' at the fun-fair in my youth, when one walked or stumbled along a wobbling platform.

As the bombers passed we moved forward again. On the ridge of the pipe-line clearing I noticed a dug-out and investigated. To my amazement it was crowded to capacity with trembling Chinese coolies. There was nothing I could do to help them and I moved on.

I think some of the bombs had dropped on A Company's position. Some more of their wounded came through our lines. There was the fantastic sight of two of these men on a delivery bicycle. The one who was more seriously wounded sat in the box on front and the other pedalled. How they kept balance was as mysterious as how they'd acquired their transport.

Firing went on for a long time. The wounded were cleared. News reached me that, while, so far, D Company had had only a few casualties, one platoon commander had been wounded. This was my friend John. While advancing with his platoon he'd had to fling himself down to take cover and a bullet passed over his shoulder, hit the back of his ankle and came out through the instep. He was removed with the other wounded and I was not to see him again for nearly a year.

While we were still returning the Jap fire and holding the crest of the pipe-line hill orders came that we were to withdraw to our original position behind the racecourse.

It wasn't, however, quite to our original position, but to a hillock between it and the racecourse. By now it was nearing the end of the day – a day which had seemed very long indeed. So far as the fighting was concerned we all felt, I think, that we'd done as well as could have been expected against an enemy who'd had the advantage of position and of air support. Losses had been heaviest in A and B Companies, who had advanced right into the Jap line of fire. Instead of throwing the invaders off the island we had had to withdraw. It didn't leave any of us in an exultant mood and finding that we were to dig in and wire all over again was rather the last straw, especially as we were so near to the tactically better line we'd prepared the previous night.

The hillock was more thickly wooded, though it was far from being dense jungle. We were still in a plantation area and very probably there'd been thinning out of trees in the immediate vicinity of the racecourse.

I moved among the men with an encouraging word. There was some grousing, with which I could sympathize. Looking back on the day, I was wondering whether it had been worth while. If we'd remained in our good defensive position and let the Japs walk into our fire the results might have been far more satisfactory. My rather gloomy thoughts were cheered by Alan Woodbridge. In some miraculous way he'd scrounged a couple of bottles of wine, the last thing one would expect to have seen in a rubber plantation.

Darkness crept over and what was to seem the longest and most terrifying night of my life started quietly enough. The rubber trees in which we were hidden had a silvery ghostly appearance in the filtering moonlight. In some strange way they seemed to serve as a blanket keeping out sound so that there was, for the most part, an eerie quietness. We could look down to the racecourse to the left, but up to the right there was a blind sector which worried us. We sent out a standing patrol to give us warning and protection from this direction. Battalion headquarters lay behind us in a sunken lane. During the evening the C.O. visited us and assured us that we in D Company didn't know how lucky we were. This drew ironic laughter, but his comment wasn't far wrong when one remembered that A and B Company had borne the brunt of the day's fighting, losing several officers and men.

Still wearing gym shoes and walking with the aid of his thumb stick, Tom moved around energetically, visiting the forward areas and then going back to battalion H.Q. for further briefings and orders.

I was left holding the fort. As platoon commanders we still had Percy and Jonah. John's platoon had been taken over by the platoon sergeant. As we had wireless and field telephones it was possible for me to keep in touch with the adjutant. There were times when his voice was wonderfully reassuring.

There was an unexpected visitor in the form of a staff officer. He was spruce right down to his polished boots. We were not smart enough for him and he made this clear, throwing in a short lecture on fortitude in adversity for full measure. He wound up with a 'backs to the wall' speech and a request to inspect the platoon positions. This provided me with my moment. I refused, and sent him off to battalion H.Q., making sure the adjutant knew what to expect.

Percy revived the old army joke. "Well, if bread's the staff of life – the life of the staff is one long loaf."

And so night fell and I stood for a time listening to the metallic voices of the insects. There seemed no other sounds near to us. I called in to Company H.Q. Percy and Jonah and the platoon sergeant who'd taken over when John was wounded had arrived safely. We were just starting our conference when all hell seemed to break out around us. The volume of fire was frightening. I sent two of the platoon commanders back to their men and asked the third to go forward and check that all was well with the standing patrol.

Shortly after, Tom returned from C.O.'s orders at battalion H.Q. and decided to go round the whole position and check what was happening. He left me with the signallers to pass back information to battalion H.Q. But there was so little I was able to report that I decided to go in search of the standing patrol. There'd been no word from them and my fear was that they'd been wiped out. I set off, with Alan, my batman, following.

Firing could still be heard from several directions. There were brief lulls and indistinct cries. We crawled up the slope. It was slow and painful. Most low-growing plants in Malaya had thorns, but scratches were preferable to being caught in a stream of bullets. We edged higher and higher, and were almost at the top of the rise when the firing stopped.

This happened as abruptly as it had started and the comparative silence which followed was uncanny. Peering ahead, I could see men moving. The air was full of acrid fumes. There was quite a Guy Fawkes Night tang, and this was possible because the Japs had a trick of firing red flares and something akin to cracker-jacks which were really rifle-fire simulators. The object, no doubt, was to scare and to give the impression they were in greater strength and, by lobbing them over us, they appeared to be behind us.

We looked about us anxiously, not sure of any identification. I was anxious, thinking we were getting ourselves completely surrounded. A figure jumped up, quite near, and started to run off, shouting, "Yagi! Yagi!" I had the immediate thought that it was Percy calling to me. It sounded just like "Reggie". Instinctively I started to rise but my batman pulled me down again. Just as well, because it quickly became apparent that the shouting man was a Jap soldier calling to one of his mates.

The lull in the fighting persisted. Scarcely daring to breathe, we kept low and looked about us. I was getting my first look at the Japanese. They seemed to be tiny men in breeches and puttees, and to be wearing coal-scuttle-type helmets. They were busy moving their dead, and so far as we could tell they were piling body on body, like so many corpse sandbags, around their position. It seemed gruesome, all the more so in the half-light.

When I was sure that no Jap was near to us I whispered to my batman, "Let's get to hell out of here."

We began to crawl back. For myself, I was fighting down an urge to get to my feet and run as fast as I could. We seemed to make painfully slow progress and I expected any moment to be caught in the wave of a Jap advance.

Somehow we reached company H.Q. unharmed. I spoke to battalion H.Q., though there was not very much I could tell them. It was obvious that our positions were seriously threatened and that the Japs had penetrated the defences in some places at least. The firing had started up again and it went on all night, becoming louder and nearer. There was still only sketchy information reaching me for passing back.

There was a bad moment when a burst of machine-gun fire went right over our heads. I could feel sticky fluid running down my left forearm and imagined I must be hit. The absence of pain was because the arm was numb, I thought. It was only as the morning light spread that I realized what had happened. The bullets had riddled the rubber tree above us and the latex was dripping down on us.

The fighting was confused, the messages that reached me often far from clear, but I passed back whatever information I could. I hadn't seen Tom or Percy and Jonah for some time. Last I knew of them was that they'd gone forward to probe out the situation. The firing seemed to be all around us, so I advised battalion H.Q. that we were almost surrounded.

With the stronger light of day our casualties were increasing and it was decided to withdraw D Company to the sunken lane where the battalion H.Q. was situated. We'd been trained to thin out by sections when faced with a withdrawal in the face of the enemy, but the niceties of the text book went by the board. We drew back as fast as we could, a platoon at a time. I was directing them and it was a grim and pitiful sight to see the wounded being helped or carried. This had to be done under constant fire, so it was hard to comfort the wounded. I didn't hear anyone complain.

It was during this withdrawal that we lost the services of our second officer. This was Jonah, who was hit in the leg. It couldn't have happened at a worse moment, because the withdrawal was proving a very tricky business indeed, with bullets seeming to come at us from all directions. At one point the man immediately in front of me was shot through the head. I tried to lift him, realized that he must have been killed instantly and left him.

I reached the sunken lane and here I tried to get the survivors reorganized. We didn't stay long, because we had orders to move back to a position called the Adam Road line. To reach this I had to lead the company through a place which came to be known as Dead Cow Wood. Evidently a number of cattle had been grazing here and had been wiped out by artillery fire. It was a gory and depressing sight, and somehow seeing dead animals upset me more than the sight of dead men. Perhaps this was because the animals had played no part in the battle and had just been slaughtered out of the blue.

Apparently all the casualties in Dead Cow Wood were caused by the Japs firing Air Burst Shrapnel Shells. This accounted for a large number of men and cattle being killed. Battalion H.Q. was most affected, resulting in the death of R.S.M. Lunn, whom I remembered with affection from the halcyon days with the 1st Battalion in Bangalore.

While we were making our way to the new line word reached us that there were some troops still getting away from the racecourse area and that their situation was getting desperate. The C.O. ordered the carrier platoon to counter-attack and rescue them. They roared into action. The carrier platoon officer was very brave, but also impetuous. We heard afterwards that he drove straight at the enemy. There was a mêlée. A Japanese officer jumped from a tree on to the carrier and severed his head with a great sweep of a Samurai sword. This was perhaps our first stark indication of the Japs' barbaric lust for killing.

We kept to the woods on the edge of the Bukit Timah Road, going towards Singapore and at last we reached Adam Road. This ran from the Bukit Timah Road to a high point which gave quite a commanding view of the surrounding countryside. Adam Road itself was a wealthy European residential road and there was a row of large bungalows with beautiful gardens. From them there was the vista of the valley which the Japs would have to cross if they made the expected frontal attack.

Immediately before occupying one of the bungalows I was outside in the road talking to Percy. A stick of mortar bombs came raining towards us leaving little craters. Troops scattered in all directions.

27

The last bomb went off between Percy and myself and his knee-cap was blown off. I rushed to him and helped him to apply his first-aid field-dressing.

He was suffering from shock and kept saying to me, "I think I'm going to faint," as I frantically tried to tie the bandage.

I said, "Don't worry about that, old soldier. I'm not hit – but I think I'm going to faint, too."

This cheered him up quite a bit. We lifted him gently on to a carrier returning from the counter-attack and so he was evacuated – our last officer platoon commander.

As we took up our position in the bungalows, briskly because we were under fire, Tom was hit, getting a shell splinter in the back.

I seemed to lead a charmed life, for I was the only officer of D Company left unwounded. However, this was borrowed time. Not that it was the moment for me to work out my personal chances. I took stock. I had as my chief support Company Sergeant Major Rice, M.M. His nickname, as a small man, was Tuppenny. He was a regular, a very brave chap, and had won the Military Medal some years before at Dam Dil on the North-West Frontier. Although he was a strict disciplinarian all the men liked him. I also had two sergeants left for platoon command, and one corporal. Thus, three of our depleted platoons I had to leave under the command of N.C.O.s, which, to their great credit, they managed very ably.

When I was able to snatch a short rest after checking all the men were in the new positions I felt rather envious of those who had been wounded and evacuated. They had honourable scars, they had done their bit and they were out of it. That they were in reality far from being out of it didn't enter my head. I was just conscious of being left behind in all the chaos and confusion. There were perpetual explosions. I didn't know what had happened to our guns but the Jap artillery were throwing over everything they could. It seemed to me that these ground-shaking explosions contributed as much to loss of stamina as lack of sleep for several nights and the scruffiness of being unwashed and unshaved.

The residence which we had selected as company H.Q. had presented a strange sight when we first entered it. The dining-room table was set for dinner. The larder was fully stocked with food and wines. Obviously the occupants had left in a desperate hurry. While the staging was right for a land version of the *Mary Celeste*, there was no mystery. We knew only too well why this beautiful home had been

28

abandoned. We'd probably, I thought grimly, be getting out with equal speed ourselves.

There was an electric stove and, when we tried this, we found it was working. As the means were to hand it was clearly worth the effort – D Company had a hot meal from the kitchen. They needed it badly and it helped to put new life into them.

The noise of battle was coming inexorably nearer. Inside the house there was a line of bullet marks on the wall opposite the large verandah window. It was amusing to see how the runners behaved. They would come in from the front door, spot the marks and go down on all fours, crawl across the room and stand up again when they reached the greater safety of the dining-room.

At this time we were still identifiable as a separate company. We'd lost all our officers but myself and the company strength must have been down to about two-thirds of its original number. A rifle company has approximately a hundred men. There were with me now some sixty odd.

At this point in the battle I think I started to lose heart, although I never mentioned it to the sergeant-major or the men. I had lost Tom, John, Percy, and Jonah, and felt the awful loneliness of command under such conditions. Nevertheless I had Tuppenny Rice, Alan Woodbridge and the N.C.O.s to back me up. In retrospect I realize I was very lucky and privileged having them and the support of the good spirit which always seemed to sustain D Company.

In spite of my forebodings I tried to cheer myself up and I found it helped to keep doing something. An instance of this was when I was awaiting orders to occupy the Adam Road line. I discussed Henry V at Agincourt with the sergeant-major while we fuzed a box of hand grenades.

Several incidents at this time served to remind me of the good morale of D Company. Apparently my nickname amongst the men was "Gus". When I went round the position I would hear someone shout "Watch it boys – here comes Gus." As I passed a voice would say, "Steady, Gus." The C.S.M. would pounce.

'Who are you talking to?"

"No one, sir," came the sharp reply.

At one position I asked the anti-tank fellow what he'd done with the anti-tank rifle.

"I've thrown it away, sir."

"Are you mad?" I said. "Put him on a charge, Sergeant-Major."

Actually the man never came up before me. The wretched weapon was a great burden in retreat and was not very effective.

On these tours round the company, besides the C.S.M. I was always followed by the faithful Alan Woodbridge. It became even a battalion joke for me to say, "Shadow me, Woodbridge. Dog my footsteps." To which he would reply under his breath, "Steady, Gus."

We seemed to have no close contact with other troops and I was not surprised when, with evening coming on, we were told to pull back. I could sympathize, though, with the men of Company H.Q. in the house, who complained that it was only done to stop anyone from snatching a bit of sleep on a real bed.

The reorganized defence line brought us into touch with other companies on either flank. We were to occupy the edge of an old quarry behind Adam Road. We couldn't use the full cover of the quarry but had to take up positions on the crest as deep as possible. It meant more digging of slit trenches. It was a restless night. There was a lot of sporadic firing and eventually the bushes around us caught fire. I felt the only thing was to evacuate. If the men stayed there they'd be roasted to death; if they tried to fight the flames they'd be wonderful targets for the Japs. I heard there was some consternation at H.Q. where the position wasn't fully appreciated.

Back we went into Adam Road. When we could see that the fire had burnt itself out we returned to the ghastly slit trenches surrounded by craters and smouldering embers. The dawn light did nothing to beautify the scene. Our nostrils still seemed to be filled with the smoke from the burning bushes.

I don't know how they managed to reach us, but there were some rumours circulating among the troops. One was that an American aircraft carrier had arrived and we should very quickly have some of the air support we'd so badly needed. Another was that a Rolls Royce with a white flag had been seen driving up the Bukit Timah Road.

One of our humorists, with Aldershot manoeuvres in mind, said this must be the chief umpire and that the exercise would soon be over.

Actually this car was conveying a truce party from General Percival to General Yamashita, going to discuss terms for a surrender.

At the time I'd no thought that anything of this nature was happening. The car with the white flag was just another story, I felt. Our position was a nasty one; we had our backs to the wall, but we were very far from beaten. There was plenty of fight left in

D Company. Given some artillery support and a reasonable defensive position, I believed they could well do their part in holding the Japanese advance until there could be reorganization in our rear and the reserves could be thrown in for a strong counter-attack.

What I didn't realize was that there were no reserves.

There were warning cries along the quarry as a solitary aircraft was sighted. Flying very low it came towards us. I could see the pilot's goggled face and I even saw him signalling by flash lamp to the Jap guns. A Bofors gun opened up on him. He was so low I fired a few shots with a rifle, but he swept past safely. His work was done only too well. The most tremendous bombardment struck us. It was like a sudden blast. The ground rocked and loose earth and stones went up in great pillars all around us. We dived into our pitifully inadequate slit trenches and tried to claw into the earth. Above the explosions I could hear the screams of wounded men. There was a blinding flash and the slit trench fell in on me. I was sinking into a black pit. Then there was darkness.

*     *     *

I came round reluctantly. It seemed so much easier to make no effort, to slip back into the darkness. I'd been for a long time without sleep. It was good to be lying down. My hands were already moving, exploring. My eyes were open. It wasn't so easy to fight against the urge to live.

I was on a stretcher. It was on a stone floor in a white-washed outhouse. The light was going. I watched it as it faded, becoming aware that there were other stretchers around me. Most of the men were lying quietly, a few were groaning. A medical orderly appeared. He didn't come near enough for me to speak. I kept trying to work out what had happened. My back was very sore, as if it had a burning rod in it. I think the pain helped me to remember the slit trench. I must have caught the blast in the back from the flying debris of rocks and stones.

At last an orderly came near. "You'll be okay, sir," he said. "We'll be moving you all to Fullerton Building in the morning. You'll be more comfortable there."

"How's it going?" I whispered.

For a moment he hesitated. Then he said, "It's all over, sir. We've surrendered."

Surrendered. I suddenly felt a bit sick. I turned my head away. I lay for a long time, trying to think clearly. What struck me so strongly was the wastage. The months of convoy. The few days of battle – and now captivity. For how long? What had happened to the battalion? How many had been killed? How many had been wounded? What had happened to Alan, my batman?

The questions poured into my mind. This was one of the blackest moments of my life. I was overwhelmed with despair and with apprehension, not just for myself but for all the men who'd served under me during the last hours of the fight. The dying light was symbolic of my own hopes and spirits. Fading out. I wished I could crawl into the darkness and be lost. I wasn't afraid of death. It would be the pleasant way out, just to sink into oblivion.

But all that happened was that I slept. My body was very, very weary.

# Chapter 4

INTO CAPTIVITY – CHANGI, SINGAPORE
FEBRUARY–JULY 1942

The normal pattern of recovery is for there to be an increasing interest in what goes on, a desire to get better quickly, to participate in living. All these were absent. I couldn't dull my brain, stop it from thinking – but I wanted to. Awareness meant being aware of defeat, of incarceration ahead. From now on and for God only knew how long, life was going to be uncomfortable and futile. Only by a miracle would I be able to do anything to improve it. So the easy way for the moment was to drift off, to hover on the brink of consciousness so that it was always possible to withdraw into oblivion.

It wasn't the mental attitude for a swift recovery; but there wasn't the medical attention either. When I awoke in the morning I was still on the outhouse floor at the casualty clearing station. I was carried on a stretcher to an ambulance and driven to Victoria Hall, a large building in the centre of Singapore. This adjoined Fullerton Building, which was the General Post Office.

It was a vast hall which had been turned into an emergency hospital and it was jammed tight with beds which almost touched each other, so that the doctors and medical orderlies only moved around with difficulty. The beds were quickly filled to capacity with wounded men, suffering varying degrees of agony, some moaning, some crying out, some ominously silent.

The medical staff were doing their best, wearing themselves out, but the situation was beyond their fully stretched capacity. It was not until the day was ending that my first and only meal in twenty-four hours reached me. It consisted of a packet of biscuits and a cup of tea.

Ministering to the near-dead and the dying, to the most serious

33

cases, kept the doctors too occupied to tend to those with slighter wounds. There was, in this make-shift hospital, one surprising sight. This was a young Chinese nurse going from bed to bed like an oriental Florence Nightingale. I marvelled a little at her loyalty, for I was sure most of her people had disowned us by now, or would at least be most careful not to identify themselves with us.

I was near an enormous arched window. There was a balcony outside, just above street level. Jap tanks rumbled by and I had my first view of the conquerors. There was a stream of vehicles carrying Japanese infantry. From my prone position it seemed they were seated on benches, rigidly at attention in a bolt upright position. They clasped rifles with bayonets fixed and they wore their coal-scuttle steel helmets with a *papier mâché* or fibre covering for protection against the sun. They looked like puppet soldiers. It astonished me that they should show no elation. Their exploits in subduing so vast an area in so short a time must surely rank as one of the most victorious campaigns in military history. Nothing in the appearance of these soldiers suggested they knew this.

My thinking at the time was very disjointed. Somehow, in spite of the sounds of suffering, I drifted at intervals into some stage between sleeping and waking. I was aroused from one of these by an orderly who told me I was being moved to a hospital in the Changi area. Any move must surely be for the better. A real hospital should mean greater comfort. Several of us were placed in an ambulance and we started the journey.

It wasn't a long one. We stopped and were carried into what appeared to be a school, judging by the desks, blackboards and easels.

Those of us who were sufficiently well to talk discussed what this could mean. Somebody grimly suggested that our re-education was to begin. Lessons in Japanese.

Why we were halted at this place we never discovered. We spent the night and in the morning were awakened with a plate of hot beans and tinned bacon. This was the first decent meal I'd had for what seemed an eternity. I tried to recall when I'd last eaten and my memory seemed fuzzy. Perhaps it was that meal in the abandoned bungalow.

At last we resumed our journey to Changi. Through the back of the ambulance I could recognize that we were travelling the same road as that taken by our Australian truck drivers the day of our arrival in Singapore. But this time there was a great difference. There was a festive appearance, though the decorative note was monotonous – just the Japanese flag. It was flying from every hut, over every kampong. The Rising Sun. Later it was generally known among the troops as 'the poached egg', but at this moment there was something overwhelming in the constant reminder of the conquerors of southeast Asia. And it looked as if the New Order in Asia was being accepted by everybody. I wondered how long all these households had possessed Japanese flags. The truth seemed to be that they'd prepared for victory by either side. When my personal ordeal was nearly over, at the end of the war just after the Japanese surrender, I came this same way again and the Union Jack was raised over every hut and kampong.

Towards the end of our journey in this ambulance we passed Changi jail. This was my second sight of the place. It was a shock to work out that I'd seen in for the first time only three weeks ago, for an eternity seemed to have passed since then.

At last we reached the centre of the Changi area. Here were the Roberts Barracks, a block of large buildings which had been turned into an enormous hospital. This was better organized and more spacious than any place I'd encountered so far; but it was quickly obvious to me that we were all in for a thin time. Every possible effort was being made to achieve normal hospital conditions, but there was a warning in the economical use of medical supplies and the smallness of the rations.

Food became an escapist topic of conversation among the patients. We worked out what meals we'd like to have if we could be free once more and back home. We rather overlooked the fact that there were shortages at home, and price didn't restrict our imaginations.

I was now making progress physically – though this would have been much faster with more nourishing and more palatable food – but my mental attitude remained much the same. There was a soul-destroying sense of failure, of having expended so much of myself in achieving nothing. And this induced a lethargy; everything seeming so much trouble that it wasn't worth doing. And when, about a fortnight later, I was discharged from the hospital and rejoined the battalion I was to find everybody else similarly affected.

The battalion was temporarily quartered in a nearby barrack block, with the troops upstairs and the officers on the ground floor. Slowly our people were filtering back from Singapore. We had the C.O. with us but even he was depressed.

This was the bitterness of defeat, unavoidable. It was a cup which had to be drained. We'd seen something of the Japs' fighting quality, we'd seen even more of our own weakness in equipment. Not even the most optimistic could envisage a sudden reversal of military fortune. Salvation might come eventually from the Americans, but their Pacific Fleet had been smashed at Pearl Harbor and it would be a long time before they could bring it back to strength and sail out against the treacherous Japanese.

There was one moment of cheerfulness, strangely enough provided by a Japanese officer who arrived one afternoon and had an official conversation with our C.O. It transpired that during the battle they were opposing C.O.s

When their talk was over our C.O. returned to us with the first smile we'd seen for a long time. He explained who his caller had been and added, "At least he admitted that some of the stiffest opposition to their advance came from the area of Bukit Timah village and the racecourse."

This had a cheering effect on us all. As we sorted ourselves out and tried to restore some sort of order we were moved from the vicinity of the hospital to a tented camp on a cricket field called the Maidan. This meant we had more room for moving around, and it eased tension a bit. The survivors from the fighting gradually came together here, until only the seriously wounded were left in Roberts Hospital. There was no sign of my friend John Hayne. I was not to learn until later what had happened to him.

He'd been wounded before the surrender and taken to Alexandra Hospital. It was here that one of the worst atrocities of the campaign took place. The Japanese afterwards claimed that Indian troops fired on them from the hospital. Whether this was true I don't know, but it was certainly no justification for what followed. The Japs overran the hospital, shooting and bayonetting staff and patients – even killing a man who was lying on the operating table. There was a further mass execution the next morning when more of the staff and patients were butchered in cold blood. John, luckily, was not among them.

What we did begin to learn at our new camp was the true face of the enemy. Our men who'd been unwounded at the time of the surrender had been rounded up and, although they were in a completely exhausted state, were forced to make the long march to captivity. The stragglers were clubbed and prodded with bayonets to keep them on the move.

The Japanese had signed a Hague Convention regarding prisoners-of-war in 1907. A later and more humane code was embodied in the Geneva Convention of 1929. The Japanese representative had signed this but his government had not ratified it. Perhaps the nearest they had to a code was Bushido, the Way of the Warrior. But its provisions were drawn up long ago. One set of rules belongs to the sixteenth century. Anyway these applied to the Samurai, and the ordinary soldier hardly qualified.

In Singapore the Japs were suddenly confronted with an army of prisoners and they didn't know what to do with them. We were to learn, the painful way, that the majority of our captors – including their officers – were of very limited intelligence and were likely to fly into a violently savage temper whenever anything went wrong or they considered themselves insulted. At such times the veneer of civilization was very thin, and underneath it there was a savage far more vicious than some of the most primitive people in the world.

Their ignorance of the West was surprising. Ostensibly Nazi Germany and Fascist Italy were their allies. Sometimes a Jap would say, "Adolf Hitler, Mussolini, very good, number one." But this seemed no more than a catch-phrase. They never mentioned the military successes of their allies and gave no sign of being interested in how they were faring. My feeling was that Britain and America represented a defeated enemy to them. The fact that they'd defeated Britain and America in the Far East, for the moment, led them to think the war was over and anything which might happen in Africa or Europe was of no importance whatsoever.

In our new tended camp the greatest privation was the perpetual gnawing pangs of hunger. We had only sufficient rice to provide a few ounces per man per day. There was one day when the rice issued to us by the Japs was polluted by some vile chemical. What chemical and how it happened I don't know. Many thought it was an attempt to get rid of unwanted prisoners by poisoning them, but there were no deaths. We finished up the tainted rice because we were so hungry.

This near-starvation increased the difficulty of rising above our misery. There were a few moments of cheerfulness, of course, especially my reunion with John, who'd not been very badly wounded. And the sergeant-major, Tuppenny, was back with us. He'd survived, fighting on his feet to the end.

We didn't feel like making efforts, but we knew it was vital to build up the morale of the men. In our present state of misery none of us was equipped to endure further ordeals.

Tom was still suffering from Singapore foot and had to go around in his old gym shoes and this was an extra burden he had to endure. I often marvelled at the way he forced himself on and on.

We started to organize games, hobbies and classes. We were met with apathy, but somehow we cajoled and bullied and managed to get things started. The sergeant-major was a wonderful help. I told him he'd have to re-impose discipline gradually and he showed great restraint.

We were to find, later, that it was the man who kept himself as clean as possible, who shaved, and who did his best to be mentally and physically alert who survived. The poor wretches who let themselves go, who traded some of their clothing for food extras, and who tried to dodge all spare-time activities, were the most likely to go under.

In the course of our 'pep' talks we kept insisting that although we'd lost the battle for Singapore that wasn't the end. We'd win the war, given time. Meanwhile, it was up to us to be ready for the day of liberation. I'm sure our audiences used to mock and profane us behind our backs, but I'm equally sure that without such efforts as we were making we'd have degenerated into a rabble.

There was one immediate benefit. We were to discover that the Japs did have a certain admiration for soldierly-looking troops and were inclined to give them a better deal. Not that this amounted to much, except in rare cases, but in our condition any concession or favour was of value.

I was fortunate to go through this period of reorganization with plenty of assistance from senior and brother officers, because later on I was to be the senior officer in a working party where conditions at times were to be really testing. This was my training.

There was a lot of clearance work to be done in Singapore and the Japs started to make use of their prisoners-of-war. We had to supply working parties. Our destination was the docks, near the spot where we had arrived. We were all keen to do this because of the change, the 'perks', and the opportunity of some brief contact with the outside world.

On my second trip we were engaged in rolling drums of petrol from the quayside to waiting rolling stock. We quickly evolved a good system of sabotaging the Jap war effort. In the morning we rolled the drums of petrol to a control dump by the waiting wagons. In the afternoon these drums were rolled up on to the wagons. It was extraordinary how many of the drums which had been sound in the morning were leaking by afternoon. The trains must have poured petrol all the way up the Malay peninsula or wherever they were going.

During the lunch break there was ample opportunity for making contact with a nearby party of Australians. We were to find that Australians had refined the buying or less legitimate obtaining of food into a fine art. We learnt a bit from them and there was some brisk trading with a horde of Chinese who had loaves, fish, tins of bully beef and other foods for sale or exchange. Fortunately British Malayan currency was still legal tender and a few of us had some left.

The result of this expedition was not outstandingly helpful to the Japanese war effort, but we had the best lunch for days and we had some valuable tinned food to eke out our near-starvation rations.

Conditions were getting worse in the Changi area because the Japanese were sending all their British and Australian prisoners there. The result was overcrowding. Food issues never seemed to cover the actual number of men and it became increasingly difficult to keep up the effort of achieving a standard of cleaniness.

The situation began to ease a little as more and more working parties were organized. One day I was called to a preliminary conference held by a lieutenant-colonel who informed me that I was to be in command of a working party of about a hundred men from the Royal Norfolk and Suffolk Regiments. We'd be going to an unknown destination in Singapore town. We had always had lorries to take us to the docks, but this time we had to walk. The lieutenant-colonel warned me that it would be a hard march. I was to have three officers from the Suffolks with me. John Scrimgeour, an old Etonian, was to act as my second-in-command and there were two younger officers named Cork and Bennett. All three backed me up wonderfully and we got along very well together in conditions which were sometimes temper-fraying.

Our 'secret' destination proved to be Havelock Road in the centre of Chinatown. The distance from Changi was about eighteen miles; not too difficult for fit troops, but we were all undernourished and it was an exacting ordeal. Not one man fell out or faltered. We started early in the morning and arrived in the evening. We were lucky with our Jap guards who were content to let us go at a reasonably leisurely pace. Some humorist suggested they were so patient because they were being paid by the hour.

Havelock Road turned out to be a series of large atap huts with two tiers of platforms on each side. There was reasonably good cook-house accommodation and the sanitary arrangements were satisfactory. We even had showers.

There was a small river and over the other side there was another large camp. This was called River Valley Road Camp. There was a bridge across the river and in the evenings we were free to exchange visits with the men in this other camp. I used to walk across with John Scrimgeour. We met an oldish man who did portrait painting. His resources were limited but he produced good likenesses of us. There was another artist, a corporal in the Cambridgeshires, who did some excellent pencil sketches of camp scenes.

There was one hut in River Valley Road Camp where it was said you could buy anything from a Bren gun to a penknife, so well was the local black market organized.

We were given a day to settle in. We felt our Japanese were being very gentlemanly and hospitable. I was not so pleased with them the next day when I found that the working companies were being re-organized and their size increased. I said that I'd prefer to retain only my original party, but it was no use. I had to take on about fifty more men. We were designated as H.W.3 Company which meant Hand Wagon Company No. 3. Our job would be to wheel rubble from the bombed sites all over Singapore town. I didn't mind the work; I could see that there would be ample opportunities for shopping and for the gentle art of fiddling. And there might be some chances of being even worse than useless to the Jap war effort.

The language barrier was always a source of mixed laughter and frustration. In one camp the Japs insisted we learn Japanese (NIPPON-GO). The Jap making this announcement could speak pidgin English as follows: "ORRU MAINE MUSK REARN JAPANESE RANGAUGE". In fact they tried to insist we only spoke Japanese to them. From then on most communication was done by sign language. One day one of our chaps asked a particularly nasty Nip a question in English and was shouted at "NIPPON-GO!! NIPPON-GO!!" [meaning 'Japanese language!'] and got the follow-ing answer: "Yes I wish you all would, and the further the better."

I was unhappy about the new men. My original party had a back-ground of good training and discipline. This was helping them to

carry on in spite of semi-starvation and without complete demoral-
ization setting in. The new men had been gathered from here and
there. The training standard was lower and what corps or regimental
loyalty they'd possessed had been broken up. Looking them over I
felt sure there were some trouble-makers. I was not unsympathetic to
dejection and a sense of nothing being worth the effort. I'd just come
through all that myself. But I knew also how important it was to snap
out of it. I decided to keep a close watch on the new men and I warned
my other officers.

Although the work was primitive and back-breaking, it was a great
opportunity to get out of camp on to the streets of Singapore and do
a bit of scrounging, as nearly all the Chinese were very friendly and
generous with gifts of bananas, pineapples, tins of food and even odd
clothes.

A most amusing sight was to see three men per hand-wagon going
down a street in a long column of carts with the British Officers and
some of the men zigzagging in and out of Chinese shops and bazaars,
with Nip sentries running after them and boxing all and sundries'
ears. The main problem was to hide all the loot in the hand-wagon
and get it past the Camp Guard Hut. The sentries with the party,
having boxed a few ears, felt honour was satisfied and allowed the
men to keep whatever they had obtained, and there appeared to be
no liaison whatever between the working party sentries and the camp
guards; in fact, an odd form of rivalry existed. When the empty hand-
wagons came back to camp at the end of the day it was organized
that an officer would march with the wagon containing the goods,
which was covered by men's discarded shirts. As the officer saluted
the Camp Guard, he would bow low so averting his gaze from the
cart to the ground, and thus it was quickly whipped past.

Whilst working on the docks moving supplies of tinned food in
crates around the warehouses, the odd crate would be toppled over
and break, scattering tins in all directions. This would result in a host
of prisoners gathering around to help the poor unfortunate and his
Jap sentry to pick them all up, and so surreptitiously help themselves.
Actually the Japs got wise to this and one day a Jap officer arrived in
a staff car plus interpreter and called everyone to attention, and gathered them around. "High Japanese officer is not happy. So much
stealing and looting is bad for Japanese Authority, over prisoners –
must stop immediately." Whilst this was going on three of our chaps
were behind the car with a rubber tube siphoning out the petrol. The

41

oration over, back to work and the staff car drove off and ran out of petrol at the end of the road.

Our immediate bosses were Jap N.C.O.s and privates. It was my first real opportunity of studying the Jap soldier. Uniforms were of poor quality, but well washed and mended. They managed to achieve a real smartness. Towards their officers they were completely obedient, perfectly disciplined. We were particularly fortunate in that these turned out to be the nicest Japs we ever met.

The best, in my experience, was a very pleasant-looking little man named Kamita. He was well mannered and softly spoken. Kamita didn't hide his sympathy for us and he seemed quite genuinely to feel for the hardships we endured. He even, in his friendliness, went to the dangerous extent of taking three photographs in Havelock Road, one of himself, two of our little group.

I don't know how far his example influenced the others, but they certainly treated us as well as they could. Our rubble-clearing took us all over the place. Sometimes we were in the centre, at Raffles Place. Sometimes we were in the narrow crowded streets of what we thought of as Singapore's China Town. Progress through these streets looked like something from a Marx Brothers film. Men would dodge in and out of the box-like shops and then dash back to the carts and hide their purchases under the rubbish. Kamita and the others must have known what was going on, but they kept up a fine pretence of ignorance.

There was an officer named Simon Thwaites from another working party who contrived one day to purchase a Union Jack. This he wrapped round his chest under his shirt. Then, feeling bored with the chores of the day, he ordered a rickshaw and in this followed up his men who were trundling the rubbish carts. Eventually a Jap sentry saw him. On the Siamese–Burma Railway such an incident would have undoubtedly involved severe punishment. Here all that happened was that the Jap gave Thwaites an admonishing look and boxed the rickshaw coolie's ears.

But if we were seeing the better side of our captors, we also had gruesome evidence of their savagery. One day we were wheeling our loads of rubble around Singapore Park when we noticed some strange round objects on the railings. A few of us went over to investigate and to our horror saw that they were human heads, severed and impaled. It was a sight which made most of us feel a bit sick. I found it so hard to believe that I asked a Jap sentry what this outrage meant.

He said, "China robber man no good eega – damme, damme." We discovered later that these were the heads of Chinese saboteurs, displayed as a warning to others. Somebody did make the comment that we'd done much the same sort of thing a few hundred years ago when heads were exposed on Temple Bar. But this was 1942 and the Japs claimed to be as civilized as the rest of us.

I had another distressing experience. One night some of the men came to me to report that there was a Chinaman tied up by his thumbs and hanging from a lamp-post just outside the camp entrance. His screaming was upsetting everybody. It seemed his poor wife and child had come along to plead at the Jap guardroom.

I felt I had to do what I could, even though I'd be trying to interfere in matters which were no business of mine. This knowledge didn't increase my confidence. As I approached the guardroom in considerable trepidation I could see the poor wretch whose agonized cries had been ringing in my ears for some minutes.

The guard commander might have been the model for a caricature of a Japanese officer. He was about as ugly as it was possible for a human to be, with a black beard and a venomous expression.

He barked at me in Japanese. Then he sent for the interpreter.

I said, "Please, for humanity's sake, release this poor Chinaman." Even while the interpreter spoke I knew I'd failed. The Jap officer looked even more furious. He started to shout excitedly. The scared interpreter turned to me and said quickly, "The officer says if you do not mind your own business, you will be strung up with the Chinaman."

I left hurriedly. There was nothing more I could say. I'd only make trouble for myself and make things even worse for the victim. "You've done what you could," I told myself, but it was small comfort. I thought that if ever I were free to renew the fight I'd like to come up against that officer in battle. I'd shoot him down without the slightest compunction.

Fortunately, other nights were not marred by such incidents and we had as good a time as was possible, considering our lot. There was the visiting between ourselves and the River Valley Road people. Pineapples, bread and tins of milk were brought round to the huts. There was even hot sweet tea at ten cents a mug. We had a bit of money because the Japs paid us in their new Japanese Malayan currency, and our own was still in circulation.

The Japanese captain in charge of Havelock Road camp was

named Naguchi. He was a posturing oriental popinjay who was always well dressed in a white shirt, riding breeches, and gleaming top boots. He had the inevitable Samurai sword. He wore thick-lensed glasses and had a small Charlie Chaplin moustache. He was crafty, but I think we constantly outwitted him. He wasn't nearly as smart as he imagined, as the following incident shows.

We were paraded one morning and he delivered an oration. The gist was that mail was being exchanged between our camp and Changi. This was true enough, since our news was scarce and our only source of information was the sick truck which made the Changi run.

Naguchi, standing on a mound of earth, was gesticulating vigorously at several of our colonels in the front row of the audience. He threatened that if this clandestine mail service continued all visits between ourselves and our friends in the River Valley Camp would be stopped, as would the sick truck to Changi.

One of our troops, who didn't know what all this was about, came on the parade ground and, completely ignoring Naguchi, stopped in front of one of our colonels, saluted and said: "Excuse me, sir – letter from Changi."

It was a tense moment. Nobody laughed or batted an eyelid. The Colonel pocketed the letter, putting on a good act of being unconcerned. And Naguchi continued his warnings. I can only think it never entered his head that such a flagrant breach of rules he was laying down would take place so openly. The Japanese were very secretive by nature, even to the extent of causing inconvenience to each other. They were also rather one-track minded. Sudden searches for some particular object were by no means infrequent, and on one occasion over in the River Valley Road Camp the guards were told to look for wireless valves. In one of the Australian huts they unearthed the spare barrel of a Bren gun. Everyone froze with fear. But Bren-gun barrels were not what the Japs were looking for, so they handed this back.

There was a sudden clamping down on our visits to the River Valley Camp and for a sinister reason as we afterwards discovered. An Australian soldier had been caught lifting tins of food from a warehouse. This went on all the time and he happened to be unlucky. He received a terrible beating up and his bleeding and battered body was tied to a tree at the camp entrance. There'd been no outrages of this nature in our camp and perhaps Naguchi felt the less we knew of the incident the better.

One morning we were, for no very obvious reason, given a day off.

We rested in our huts. Kamita arrived at mine and beckoned to me, so I joined him outside.

"You like walk?" he asked.

I said, "Yes."

It was a very strange experience. I walked at his side and he took me out of the camp past the guardroom. We walked round the streets of Singapore, just like two friends in peacetime. I felt free again. It was wonderful. Of course there was the constant reminder of reality. There were Jap officers obviously having a spell off duty and some Jap sailors. Nobody took the least bit of notice of me. I could only presume that this was because there were a number of European neutrals who were allowed to move around unmolested: Swiss, Irish, Swedes, and so on.

We finished our outing by going into a coffee-shop and having a real cup of coffee with real sugar. It was unbelievable. Why Kamita showed me this kindness was a mystery, but if ever there was a good Jap he was one.

We had another friend of a different nationality. He was a Chinaman named Ki Yat. He was a tall, thin man, rather humorous-looking. He had a few teeth missing, their places taken by gold ones. Perhaps he had some strong personal reason for hating the Japs. He certainly took alarming risks to cheer us up and give us oddments of food. He would appear alongside a working party, hand over a tin of food and vanish. Sometimes he walked beside our column as we were on the march, talking out of the corner of his mouth and giving us the news. Unfortunately most of it was exaggerated, much of it being sheer rumour. He told us the Allies had landed in Penang and were advancing down the mainland. Alas, there was no truth in this. But we forgave him. One day he managed to give me a sack full of tinned food. Another time he managed to take John Scrimgeour's shoes to the cobblers for repair. He appeared and disappeared like an Oriental Scarlet Pimpernel, and his various exploits cheered us almost as much as the food he handed over.

The thought crossed my mind more than once that he might be a Chiang Kai-shek agent, or some manner of secret service man. When I was back in Malaya after the war I made a point of visiting the Havelock Road district and inquiring for Ki Yat. This was in 1950. Nobody admitted having heard of him. I tried the various shops he'd so often frequented but he'd completely vanished. Perhaps my old suspicion was right.

I've said that we were fortunate in our Japanese guards. Of course we had special names for them, not entirely complimentary but which they seemed to enjoy. There was Laughing Charlie, Flip the Frog, Bill Sykes the Burglar, and Plug Ugly. One guard was a member of the Tokyo Salvation Army and had photographs of himself in Salvation Army uniform along with his wife and little daughter. It was inevitable he should be called Holy Joe, which always made him grin. But one day he asked me, "What is Joe? Is it good?"

I reassured him. "Yes. Joe Louis – good boxer. Joe Stalin – good dictator." (Of course Stalin was our ally by this time.) I finished by saying, "Your To-Joe – you think him very good."

Holy Joe was satisfied. Tactfully, I'd given my opinion of Tojo under my breath.

# Chapter 5

## WORKING PARTIES IN SINGAPORE, CHANGI
## JULY 1942–APRIL 1943

I celebrated my birthday – 21st June – at the Havelock Road camp. We had the celebration in the officers' hut and each one present had a fried egg. Our diet was so far reduced that this was the best we could manage, and indeed seemed a banquet at that time.

Shortly after this orders came that we were to move to a place called Tanjong Rhu. There was a grand reshuffle of officers and men because Nos 2 and 3 hand-wagon companies were amalgamated. This roughly doubled our strength and gave us a new C.O. in the person of Humphrey Hyde, a major in the Manchesters. All my officers had been from the Suffolks, but now we had extra officers and men from what were known as Divisional Ancillary Troops – such people as Signals, R.A.S.C. and so on.

Tanjong Rhu is a peninsula jutting out into the sea beyond Kallang Airport. It had been a Chinese slum district and had suffered from bombing. The village was at the end of a long narrow road which ran round three sides of the airport. The houses of this Chinese version of a shanty town were deserted. The shops were derelict. We never heard what had become of the inhabitants. Perhaps they'd all run away, or the Japs may have evicted them.

We had an upstairs room in one of the houses as an officers' quarters. The sergeants were next door, and the men were quartered in the rest of the village. We were to spend a few months here, still moving rubble, but with the difference that now we dumped it into the sea, ostensibly to make a wharf. Naturally we were far from constructive in the manner of our dumping.

There was a sea wall, and when the day's work and the roll call were over, it was very pleasant to sit on this, staring seawards. It was also frustrating. We knew that to the south lay Australia and freedom, but it was as unattainable as the moon. This had been a fishing village, but all the boats had been taken away by the Japanese. Escape was impossible. There was only one way into the village, except by water, and this was controlled by a Jap guardroom. We were closely checked each night at *tenko*, or roll-call. All the fit men were paraded in the village street, and the sick where they lay in their houses. This checking was conducted by a squad of one-star Japanese privates. This appeared to be the lowest form of life in their army, for they frequently had their ears boxed by their two-star compatriots.

We still had our original working party guards, including our friend Kamita. They were under the command of a warrant officer named Yoshioko. He was a kindly little person and Kamita seemed to be his right-hand man.

As I was "Number One" of the amalgamated hand-wagon companies I was fortunate in having such men as these to deal with. There was never an ugly incident, no ear boxing, no cross words.

One evening after roll-call Yoshioko, accompanied by Kamita, came into the officers' quarters. I tried to explain to him that many of the men were complaining of bed bugs. I wanted to appeal to him for any help he could give. Unfortunately I had to rely a great deal on sign language, and after a dozen or so attempts Yoshioko still looked mystified. Then suddenly a gleam of recognition came into his eyes and he proceeded to imitate a bed bug by moving sideways and flailing his arms like a crab. His antics produced such a roar of laughter from everybody there that the Jap guard turned out to investigate. I'm convinced that it was only Yoshioko's presence which saved us from a round of face slapping.

Normally we were troubled very little in the evenings. John Scrimgeour had a portable gramophone and we often used to sit in the dark listening to his invaluable collection of some dozen records.

We were plagued by sand flies, tiny winged insects with a pin-prick bite. They were so light that if you slapped at one the current of air created by your hand swept them away to safety. As a result of the bites I went down with dengue fever. I seemed to ache all over. Our M.O. was a Welshman called Dai Davies. He was ever cheerful, even turning his lack of medical supplies into a joke. His advice was always, "Stick around – and drink a gallon of water a day."

There was nothing else he could recommend for us to drink. But what he couldn't give us medically he more than made up for by his light-hearted spirits. A visit from him always cheered up the patient. He was a human tonic and invaluable.

I was ordered to remain in bed. I could look out on Kallang airport. But it was frustrating to see 'planes leaving the ground so easily, especially as the most regular of them all was a Lockheed Hudson. It flew a routine patrol at dawn and dusk. It never failed to take off, and it was so well on schedule we could tell the time by it.

I heard later of a daring attempt to escape in this 'plane. A party of Australians worked daily on the airstrip and among them was an R.A.A.F. officer who'd not actually flown Hudsons but reckoned he could manage to get one off the ground. A chance came one day. They stopped for a rest alongside the 'plane which was only guarded by one Jap sentry. He was far from alert, snoozing or daydreaming, and the Australian and some of the others managed to creep past him and enter the 'plane. But it was a vain effort. The pilot, being unfamiliar with the machine, didn't know the position of the controls and everything in the cockpit was marked in Japanese, right down to the instruments. The attempt had to be abandoned. It would have taken too much trial and error and far too long.

We still had the sick truck which went from Tanjong Rhu to Havelock Road and then on to Changi taking our worst cases. We were now reaching six months of a completely rice diet and the deficiency diseases such as beri-beri and pellagra were rife. The sufferers needed treatment in Roberts Hospital. On each trip the sick truck carried as much clandestine mail as possible.

It was through this medium that we received some distressing news from Changi. The Japanese had issued an order that all prisoners of war in South-East Asia must give an undertaking not to try to escape and each man was to sign an individual paper to this effect.

There was a wholesale refusal. The Geneva Convention laid down that it is a prisoner's duty to try to escape and that to demand a promise not to escape was a contravention. The Japanese were angered and took drastic action. This was subsequently known as the Selerang Incident.

The Japs rounded up all the troops in the Changi area who were capable of moving. There were several thousand. They were marched to some buildings designed to house a battalion and were crowded into these. The ensuing privations were appalling and somewhat reminiscent of the Black Hole of Calcutta.

The senior British officer in the area was a Lieutenant-Colonel Holmes, a battalion commander of the Manchester Regiment. All those of higher rank, the generals, brigadiers, and full colonels, had been sent to Formosa. He took a bold and wise decision which undoubtedly saved countless lives and restored a rapidly deteriorating relationship between the victors and their prisoners. He ordered all men to sign the necessary papers, taking the full responsibility on his own shoulders. In law it is common knowledge that proof of duress renders the signatures as worthless. The Japs were obviously unaware of this.

Had the deadlock persisted the Singapore working parties, like our own, would have come up against the same dilemma. I'm sure Colonel Homes's decision was a wise one.

Apart from this bad news, the interminable rice diet and the increasing sickness, the days in Tanjong Rhu passed comparatively quietly and happily. For me, and many others, they came to an end with the receipt of orders that we were to send a detachment to a quarry on the west side of Singapore Harbour. This place was called Pasir Panjang.

The amalgamated H.W.2 and H.W.3 companies were now reduced in numbers and I was detailed to be in command. The main party was to stay on in Tanjong Rhu under Humphrey Hyde. So this meant reluctant leave-takings. I viewed the move with grave misgivings. My party would be changing its Jap guards for new ones. It was too much to hope for another Yoshioko, another Kamita. In this I was only too right. We were in fact, like Uncle Tom, to be sold to a new set of slave masters, one of whom was to turn out to be even worse than Simon Legree.

I had a farewell talk with Humphrey, who'd arranged that I could take Peter Tomlinson, an R.A.M.C. lieutenant, with me as medical officer. He also said that I could send back by truck if I needed help in any way.

I was very lucky still to have with me my original batman. Poor Alan Woodbridge was much thinner now. Our jokes and pleasantries and old familiar catch-phrases such as "Shadow me, Woodbridge, dog my footsteps" were becoming fewer and further between. Woodbridge was becoming a shadow himself.

My new M.O. was to become a personal friend and adviser. It was as well we had him with us, because we were to be so isolated in the months which lay ahead. He had been in the Malayan Medical

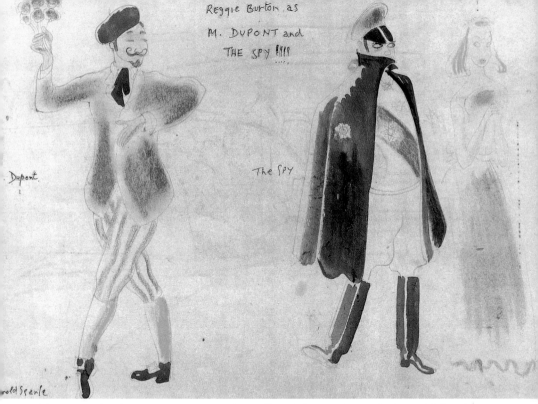

Reggie Burton as
M. DUPONT and
THE SPY !!!!

Dupont

The SPY

Ronald Searle

1. Characters in the concert party at Syme Road Camp drawn by Ronald Searle.

2. Looking down the River Kwai from the Wampo Viaduct. *(Sears Eldredge)*

3. The iron bridge at Tamarkand, made in Java under Japanese supervision and erected by POWs. *(Sears Eldredge)*

4. Looking across the bridge.

5. View from a train crossing the Wampo Viaduct after the war. *(Sears Eldredge)*

6. Another view from the Wampo Viaduct which was built by POWs. *(Sears Eldredge)*

7. Sunset over the River Kwai. *(Sears Eldredge)*

8. The cemetery at Kanchanaburi.

Service. He had great advantages over his colleagues, having practised medicine in Malaya before the war, knowing the country and speaking Malay fluently.

The severe appearance of Pasir Panjang was an omen of what was to come. It was a long quarry set between sheer rising ground on each side and leading down to a jetty. In the centre there was a large atap-roofed hut which housed approximately ten officers and two hundred and fifty men, cheek by jowl. The job consisted of hewing solid rock from the cliffs, loading it in little trucks on rails and wheeling these to the jetty. Here we tipped the rock into barges which went back to Tanjong Rhu with this material for the construction of the jetty on which we'd originally worked.

The work was too heavy for men already weakened by near-starvation diet. The heat in the quarry was gruelling. It added up to a very severe test.

I'd cut my knee badly one day on a rusty nail. Owing to my physical condition it naturally turned septic. It took a long time to heal and developed into a tropical sore. Peter Tomlinson dressed it and gave it a great deal of care and attention. I told him not to bother so much about it.

He said, "We can't afford to lose our leader, because without him this near rabble would degenerate into complete anarchy."

This amused the other officers, but there was some shrewd truth behind the joke. The trouble lay with the extra troops who had joined our regimental men from time to time. The Norfolks and Suffolks had a sense of loyalty to their regiments and this seemed to give them a reserve of strength. If ever regimental tradition and discipline paid off it was during this period of adversity. Unfortunately many of the other men who'd joined us had had much less training and they were inclined to be resentful of authority.

Although they were a headache to me, I could understand their feelings. They felt they were fragments of a unit and were being chucked around. They had to take their orders from officers who were complete strangers. General conditions were bad. The fittest among us would, back home, have been sent to a rest camp to recuperate. Instead we were doing hard manual work in intense heat and on next to no food. Energy diminished each day, and even quite small tasks became immense labours. It was easy to slip into slackness and apathy. Personal smartness became more and more difficult as our clothes wore out. We never received any from the Japs and, as an example of how we had to make do and mend, when we were freed in 1945 my shorts had accumulated no fewer than thirty-six patches. It was a wonder they were still in one piece.

But to return to the problems of command. When I felt morale was getting dangerously low I used to call the men together and we'd have a discussion. Often it was impossible to redress grievances, but airing them seemed to relieve the tension, and frequently misunderstandings could be cleared up.

I called one of these meetings when I began to sense an unusual undercurrent of resentment against the officers. This was something which had to be brought out into the open and at last the malcontents found a spokesman who said, "We agree the officers supervise us – but we do all the work – and they get extra rations."

I'd anticipated something of this nature and so I had my reply ready.

"If the officers were to give up supervision and do whole time manual labour – just like the rest of you," I said, "we'd lose our military identity. We'd become just a big labour gang with Japs as our supervisors." I made it clear that this was a state of affairs I would resist to the bitter end. "Would you want to see your officers pushed into the ranks and to have Japs take over from them?" I challenged. I reminded them that we acted as a buffer between them and the Japs. I added, "Hardly a day has gone past when I've not seen an officer take off his shirt and lend a hand."

I felt that I had the men with me, so I was able to end on a lighter note. I said, "Underneath my attitude of studied nonchalance, calculated indifference, and apparent laziness, I am conserving my energy to meet any dire contingency which may arise." This made them laugh and there was a noticeable easing of tension.

I knew from experience how swiftly suspicions over the meagre rations could spread. I shared with Doc Tomlinson and John Scrimgeour whatever extras it was possible to obtain by barter – though there were few opportunities for adding to our daily quota of rice. We did have a tin of onions, which we shared out in order to add a bit of flavour to the rice, and on one occasion my friends believed I had taken one more onion than they'd received. To this day I don't think I was guilty but I felt, as senior officer, that it was better to admit guilt for the sake of peace and quiet, and to prevent suspicion poisoning our normally happy relationship. I argued that it was impossible to share onions of varying sizes with absolute equality. We'd have to devise a method of weighing them if we were going to be so meticulous. It was an absurdly small incident but it caused a rift between us which was not healed for several days.

With this experience behind me I was anxious to cope with the accusation about rations. As officers we shared the cook-house with the men but ate separately. I came straight out with the proposal that the men should nominate a representative. He would, I said, be perfectly free to watch us eat and to check on our rations.

The men didn't take me up on this, and when I appealed to them to remember we were all British and to stick together there was a good response. "I didn't ask for you chaps to come with me – and I'm sure you didn't ask to join the party. It's hell for us all – but let's make a go of it. Don't let the Japs get us down."

After this meeting the men certainly tried hard and there was a marked improvement. I strongly suspected that the Japs were making the situation as difficult as possible for their officer prisoners. They broke up efficient units and kept demanding more and more working parties. Our senior officers had to do what they could to meet the demands and their task was made more difficult because the Japs would never say what type of work had to be done, or even where the men were to go. It was perhaps inevitable there should be muddles and that men should be parted from their proper officers. I think all the working parties were commanded by infantry regimental officers, while corps and other unit commanders were left in the Changi area without their men and with nothing to do. This state of affairs applied even when it came to providing officers for the Siamese railway; to a worse extent, actually, because wounded and lame officers were sent while comparatively fit staff and other officers were left at Changi.

My forebodings about our new Japanese overseer were all too correct. He was a junior warrant officer and an ugly-looking specimen. He had a broken nose and his general appearance suggested he'd come from a Tokyo boxing booth. We never knew his name, but we called him Damme-Damme because that was his invariable reply to our requests. What Damme-Damme means precisely I never discovered, but I think it is Japanese for "It's all hopeless. Don't ask any more." He was always followed by an interpreter whom we christened Whining Charlie. He was a cringing man with a wrinkled face reminiscent of a pickled walnut. He wasn't a Jap, but a Korean of mixed ancestry. We thought he looked and sounded like a eunuch from a Japanese whorehouse and we felt he was more an interrupter than an interpreter. He seemed scared stiff of his masters and we were sure he only translated what was likely to please Damme-Damme. Anything likely to annoy was garbled.

I had an unpleasant brush with Damme-Damme. One evening, coming back from a hard day in the quarry, I poured some clean water into a canvas bowl and then went to get a towel, though rag would have described it more accurately. When I returned, Damme-Damme was coolly standing at my bowl washing himself. I waited until he'd finished. He left the bowl, so I emptied it, poured out some clean water and started to wash. Suddenly Damme-Damme turned and leapt at me, striking me heavily across the face with his fist. He rained several more blows. He was in a rage and I was trembling with anger myself. I kept my head though, and demanded the interpreter. Damme-Damme dipped a chamois leather in the water and began to flick my face with it. This was every bit as painful as the blows. I knew that if I retaliated, I'd probably be sentenced to death for striking one of my Japanese masters.

By this time quite a crowd had gathered. I knew that Damme-Damme was trying to discredit me in front of my men and this knowledge helped me endure the ordeal. The men stood silent, glaring at my Jap tormentor.

Whining Charlie appeared. I said, trying to keep my voice steady, "Why has this man struck me like this?"

There was a long, barking discussion in Japanese. Then Whining Charlie said, "You insult him by not washing in his water. In Japan all people share bath water."

I said firmly, "In England this is not so. It is an insult to share bath water."

There was more talk between Whining Charlie and Damme-Damme. Then, as suddenly as it had started, it was over. They turned and walked away. I resumed my interrupted wash, but with more consideration for my tingling and smarting face.

In fact my face had traces of blood, as the cloth Damme-Damme had used was a chamois leather, which, cracked like a whip, had drawn fine pencil lines of blood across my face. Although no major injury was suffered any minor cuts or abrasions usually turned septic in our emaciated state and took a long time to heal.

Later I thanked the men for their moral support. This incident, like others of a similar nature, brought officers and men closer together to an astonishing degree. I'm sure the Japs were trying to break our morale, but their methods had the opposite effect. They were unpleasant enough at the time, but I urged my officers to bear any ordeal stoically because the effect on the troops would be better than any number of "pep" talks.

I always felt that Damme-Damme was as obstructive as possible, but the situation was made worse by the bad work of Whining Charlie as interpreter. We often became hopelessly bogged down. On one occasion I tried to find out, through Whining Charlie, whether there was any way we could obtain cigarettes for the troops. There was a long argument between the Jap warrant officer and the Korean interpreter and finally I received the answer that "You may smoke in the evenings provided you use an ash tray." In happier times I'm sure Damme-Damme and Whining Charlie could have made a fortune on Broadway or touring the halls as a couple of knock-about comedians. Unfortunately for us, they were not so funny at the time.

Another time I put forward a request I received the following answer, given in all seriousness: "You Burton Tyee (Captain) all time talkee-talkee – no workee."

The reply, getting around, caused much amusement. Doc Tomlinson clapped me on the back and said, "Well, don't worry, Burton Tyee. After the war they'll probably make you Viscount Pasir of Panjang." This absurd title stuck for a long time.

The best time of day was when the cool of the evening brought relief, when we knew there were some hours of rest before the labours and torments of daily life in the quarry would be resumed. When there was a moon it seemed very large and near, tempting us to sit in a small circle talking of home, or listening to John Scrimgeour's gramophone. He preferred classical music, but my favourite out of our small collection was the only tango. So when I could control the programme we had 'La Rosita' ad nauseam.

John's polished sophistication was one of our joys, especially as he treated the Japs with a sarcastic tolerance. He often managed to score off them. On one occasion we had to fill up a new form which called for details of our civilian profession or job. John wrote: Dilettante. The form wasn't returned to him, and we speculated delightedly on the perplexed Japanese staff officers who were probably trying to discover what it meant without betraying their ignorance.

We were still working in the quarry on November 11th. I managed to organize a Remembrance Day Parade. It was voluntary, but all ranks turned up, and I felt that this was an encouraging sign of the improved spirit among them. During the proceedings I read some passages from *The Book of Common Prayer*. Surprisingly, the Japs seemed to be impressed by our little ceremony and when it was over one of the guards asked me what it was all about. I told him it was First World War Remembrance and that in those days his country had been our ally. He appeared to understand.

It was difficult to provide entertainment for the men. We tried a swimming gala at the end of the jetty. I think everyone enjoyed it but we were all tired and thin, incapable of great exertion. In fact, sport was out. It would take too great a toll. Apart from that, if we did manage to rush around I feared the Japs would use that as an excuse to call for more work each day.

While we laboured in the quarry one morning we saw a handsome liner. She seemed to glide past the end of our jetty on course for Singapore harbour. We learnt later that she was an exchange vessel, the *Tatuta Maru*, bringing Red Cross supplies from South Africa. From past experience we expected nothing, but to our amazement the day came when we received a Red Cross issue. It was like manna from Heaven; but even when eked out to a minimum issue per day it only lasted two weeks.

When the Japanese took over the occupation and administration of Singapore and Malaya, they decided to rename *The Singapore Times The Shonan Shimbun*. It was to continue to be published in English and would be used as a propaganda medium, with a smattering of inaccurate and one-sided versions of the progress of the war.

In future, they decreed, the newspaper would be the organ of the Greater East Asia Co-prosperity Sphere and they hoped it would influence the opinions of all those who were left and had not been placed in prison or internment camps, such as neutral citizens of Ireland, Sweden and Switzerland, Anglo Indians and Eurasians. Copies were also issued to Prisoners of War and were gladly received for a good laugh and, if required, as toilet paper!

One story which it was hoped would illustrate the beneficence of Japanese rule ran as follows:

## BRIDES FOR SOUTHERN REGIONS

"A select Committee has been appointed in Tokyo to recruit an elite body of young ladies to go to Shonan as brides for the officials of the New Regime. They have been specially selected after having had their particulars taken down, their credentials closely scrutinized and given a stiff entrance exam."

There was no doubt whose side the Editor was on; his leading articles were in great demand and gave the P.O.W.s much-needed shafts of humour and a good laugh all round. Eventually the articles dried up and one could only assume that the poor devil of an Editor had been carted off by the dreaded Kempei-Tai (Secret Police) to one of the torture chambers in their headquarters at the notorious Outram Gaol.

In another issue it stated that the glorious Japanese Navy had won the sea battles of Midway and Coral. The entire Allied Navies, it announced, had been sunk. It was too spectacular a claim for us to believe it. I suggested we'd be nearer the truth if we turned the ship casualties the other way round.

The propaganda in the newspaper was crude and stupid. What had started as the Greater East Asia Co-Prosperity Scheme was a shambles in Singapore, where everybody appeared to be near starvation. but *Shonan Shimbun*'s 'Roving Reporter' wrote:

"Everywhere in this thriving hub of activity business is booming and trade is on the upgrade."

I think the next paragraph was stupidity and not sabotage. It ran:

"It was only yesterday that we received a report from Palm Oil Vendors in Singapore that they had never sold so much palm oil to counter vitamin deficiency in all their trading experience."

The headlines frequently provided us with a good laugh. One of the best ran this way:

IMPERIAL JAPANESE NAVY SINKS
  2 USA BATTLESHIPS
  3 USA CRUISERS
  6 USA DESTROYERS

All had arrived safely in port.

Some of the rumours which circulated proved, unfortunately, only too true. There were very strong ones about large PoW movements up-country from Singapore, and also of great numbers being shipped to Japan. Following the rumour came the reality. A contingent of our own amalgamated H.W.2 and H.W.3 companies was ordered to proceed overseas. Among those who were to go was my friend and batman Alan.

Generally we had a few days warning before such moves, but this was virtually overnight. I tried hard to keep Alan Woodbridge with me, but the Japs were adamant. He was on the list and he had to go.

This was a great blow to me. He had been with me for over two years. In strange and difficult circumstances he'd been one of my best friends, always ready to help, always dependable, always cheerful. I felt that his departure would weaken me.

When we did actually part he seemed resigned to going. There was the consoling thought that in Japan (for we believed this was where he was bound) the climate and conditions might be better. As a parting gift I presented him with my last valuable possession – my silver cigarette case. I urged him to use it for acquiring food if things ever became desperate.

I had no news of him until the end of the war, when I learnt that he'd died in Formosa. I met his widow on my eventual return to England. Alan Woodbridge was a gallant fellow – it was he who'd brought my unconscious body from the quarry top as the battle for Singapore neared its disastrous end. And here we were in a quarry again, saying goodbye.

The men who'd been selected by the Japanese for this overseas posting were all tradesmen. They were paraded and a truck from Tanjong Rhu picked them up to take them to the docks. We were desperately short of medical supplies; but there were a few we could get from Tanjong Rhu. I knew the trucks would spend the night there and return the next morning. These trucks were our usual link with the outside world.

I asked if anyone would like a trip to Tanjong Rhu, returning the next day, and a man named Thompson volunteered. I instructed him to sit in the cab with the driver, and I told him what supplies I needed and how he was to obtain them.

My plan went wrong, as the truck driver told me the next day. It seems that when the Japs counted the departing men on the dockside they found they were one short. So they collared poor Thompson, who had only the rags he stood up in. He was bundled aboard ship with the others.

It was typical of a Nipponese roll-call.

Although only the one contingent of men was taken from us at Pasir Panjang our numbers had been steadily decreasing as a result of sickness. The sick truck, which did the rounds, was kept busy. The one bright feature of this was that it did keep us in touch with the world outside the quarry. Without it we'd have felt completely isolated. Even so, the news which came to us was fragmentary and never reliable.

However, we gathered that the Japs were clearing all prisoners out of Singapore Island and setting them to work on the Greater East Asia Co-prosperity Plan, whatever that might mean. Large parties were leaving by cargo ship and, by all accounts, in the most hellishly filthy and cramped conditions. I realized, as the reports built up, that our prisoner-of-war status was little more than a formality – we were virtually slave labour.

Not all our men, though, were going in these hell ships. Enormous parties had been sent by train up-country. Their destination was unknown. There was some vast project on, because hordes of other prisoners, mostly Dutch and Javanese, were coming to Singapore. Some of these poor wretches were carried ashore in a truly desperate condition. They were under-nourished and disease-ravaged. Discipline had broken down completely and the Japs treated them like animals, herding them – even the sick and the dying – into cattle trucks for the journey up-country.

Discussing this among ourselves, we officers realized that wherever these poor devils finally camped, there could be little improvement in their conditions or their ability to make the best of things.

I urged how important it was that we should keep up the morale and discipline of our own troops. We had weekly meetings at which I talked to the men, and I was always stressing the need for making sure we didn't lapse into slovenliness and eventual degradation. The news of the working parties strengthened my case and I did feel I was putting over my ideas. My great fear was what would happen if the men suddenly found themselves deprived of leadership. I was prepared to get myself disliked and regarded as the biggest bore east of Suez if only I could achieve something which would help to preserve them from sinking into a scarcely human rabble.

We continued toiling in the quarry, never knowing what would happen to us the next day. Where would we find ourselves? In a northbound cattle truck? In the stinking hold of a cargo ship sailing for Japan?

When orders finally came it was for a very short move indeed – no farther than Serangoon Road Camp. On top of my relief at returning to a larger formation there was the cheering discovery that the Senior British Officer, Lieutenant-Colonel Prattley, was an old friend of mine. He was a battalion commander in my own regiment, though he was in another brigade. This splitting up can easily happen because a regiment may have any number of battalions and these can be anywhere. While we suffered in captivity some of our regiment was still fighting, not only in Burma, but in Italy and, later, in Normandy.

Eric Prattley had nearly all the survivors of his own battalion (the 5th Royal Norfolks) at Serangoon Road. This gave them the edge over everybody else because they were complete with officers, warrant officers and N.C.O.s, and so the sense of being a complete unit was very strong indeed. And this spirit was reflected in material things. There were, of course, no luxuries, but everything was kept as smart and clean as possible. The camp was a paradise compared with the slummy appearance of Havelock Road, Tanjong Rhu and Pasir Panjang. The malcontents in my party grumbled about coming back to what they called "Bloody Aldershot Serangoon", with its bugle calls and parades. I was not slow to draw their attention to the comparatively good health record in this camp.

There was very little trouble with the Japs. Eric Prattley's opposite number was named Yamida, who seemed a reasonable man. We were, generally speaking, fortunate in the early days of captivity because most of the Japs in charge of working parties were fighting troops, who seemed to have a certain respect for a defeated enemy. We were to see all too much of the other side of the Japanese character later, when we came up against troops who were not of front-line calibre.

At Serangoon Road we spent the first Christmas of our captivity, and it was as happy as was possible under the circumstances. A great contrast between traditional Christmas fare and what we received would be hard to find. As we were beginning to discover, it was only along the non-material lines that we could maintain what was familiar. It became more valuable, and I think this was partly the reason why the Christmas Eve Holy Communion, for which there was a record attendance, was one of the finest and most moving divine services I have ever attended. Padre Duckworth, who had been a Cambridge cox, was a wonderful man and we owed a lot to him for his selfless efforts to help us all. And in this particular celebration I believe he was instrumental in increasing our fortitude.

An example of the quite good relationships between us and our guards was the amusement created by carrying out a new Japanese order that on *tenko* (roll-call) we were to report our companies in Japanese. I had to learn by heart a recitation of this type: Dai nona san yo tye (Number 7 company) Sawyen hyaku ku me (Total 109) Genzi hyaku hachi me (Present 108) Uchi canja-byoki ichi me (Sick 1).

I doubt whether I'd have gained a diploma for pronunciation, judging by the laughter of the Jap guards when I tried to say my piece.

There is another aspect of the report which I've just quoted – the small number of sick. Later we were to be up against a very different ratio, with figures almost reversed. For the moment, though, we were able to benefit from this well-run camp. Although it was predominantly 5th battalion, while I was of the 4th, I knew most of the officers. I suppose what was left of my H.W.2 and H.W.3 parties – a mixture of 4th Norfolks, 4th Suffolks, and the odd troops who'd joined us – must have looked a very mixed bag. In a surprisingly short time, though, they absorbed us and there was the feeling of belonging to a regiment.

Between Christmas and New Year's Day we were moved again. This time transport took us back to the Changi area. This was still a main PoW camp. It was the eastern corner of Singapore Island and, in addition to the jail, the Roberts barracks and hospital, there were other sub-areas like the Maidan and the Garden and Wood areas. The entire area was sealed off with formidable barbed wire and there were plenty of Jap sentries. Once inside, movement was permitted between the sub-areas by use of the Japanese flag or emblem. There were checkpoints, but these were only lightly manned.

Our short stay in Serangoon Road had refreshed us from the rigours of the quarry, and our return to Changi was quite happy, especially as it meant meeting up with old friends. The number of prisoners inside the area had been depleted by the overseas parties as well as by those who had departed for some mysterious destination up-country, but there were still many left, including those discharged from the Roberts Hospital.

I went, with other officers, to a house in Quadrant Road. It was a semi-detached house with a sitting-room, dining-room and kitchen downstairs. Upstairs there were three bedrooms plus a bathroom. "Just like a house in Wimbledon," someone said.

There was something incongruous, especially as in some respects we behaved in a suburban manner, even to tending the small garden and clipping the front hedge.

In the evening we could stroll along Quadrant Road, drop in on friends and neighbours, or watch them playing bridge seemingly without a care in the world. At such moments it was difficult to believe that we were helplessly in the power of a barbaric people. There was, of course, the insistent voice of our hunger: the food situation seemed to go from bad to worse. I still had with me the last tin I'd received from Ki Yat. I opened it and we mixed it with the rice on New Year's Eve.

As cases of beri-beri and pellagra had increased so greatly, the Japs had been prevailed upon to issue rice polishings. These contained the husks which were a source of the necessary Vitamin B. These polishings looked, and tasted, exactly like sawdust, and the great problem was how to swallow the stuff. We tried everything we could imagine and in the end were forced to the expedient of mixing the polishings with water and somehow swallowing the lot.

A big moment for me was a reunion with John Hayne, though I was shocked by how ill and pale he looked. It had taken from February to November for his wounded ankle to heal, and even now he walked with a limp. But if I was shocked by his appearance, so he must have been by mine.

Percy, the other platoon commander, was still in hospital. We were able to visit him. He looked pale and ill and was very thin. In addition to his wounded knee-cap he'd contracted diphtheria and had come very near to death. At the hospital they were doing everything they humanely could for their patients, but for the doctors and other staff it was a perpetual and hopeless battle against shortages of both medical supplies and food.

During this period at Changi a camp concert party was active. They managed to put on a variety show and also a production of *Journey's End*.

But it was not all visiting and killing time in the most enjoyable manner that happened to be possible. Our detachment commander, a Major Monty Smythe, informed me that I was to be 'Hygiene Officer' and that I was to attend a course. This was run by the R.A.M.C. I learnt so much about vermin, lice, bed bugs and other unpleasant creatures that I used to have nightmares about them. But this duty did give me a purpose. I became too busy organizing the unit's hygiene to be able to sit around and gloom. What I was learning was to prove very valuable in the dark days that lay ahead.

Meanwhile the immediate problem was to delouse bundles of clothing belonging to the troops. High-pressure steam was the answer. I had a very ingenious chap, a Corporal Matthews from my battalion, attached to me for this work. He was a jolly person with a broad, infectious smile and a talent for invention.

We looked around and were in luck. We found an old boiler from a donkey engine. Then we hunted enthusiastically for lengths of piping and tin barrels. Eventually we were able to rig this lot into what I'm sure was the finest delouser in South-East Asia. I used to sigh after it in the days to come.

The general appearance of our washing machine may not have been impressive; perhaps it was rather a mixture of Emmet and Heath Robinson. Onlookers seemed to find it amusing and delighted in starting false alarms of steam leaks. But the delousing went on, very efficiently. Every morning we would fill the boiler, screw down the safety valve and light the wood fire. Then we had to watch a gauge for the moment when the pressure was right. As soon as this happened we rushed to open the steam cocks so that the steam could circulate among the old ragged clothing in the tin barrels.

No doubt that it was a primitive gadget, or that an expert would have constructed something less comic in appearance, but it worked, it was doing something useful and, while it didn't sound a very impressive job, I did take a pride in it.

Because of the hygiene work I was able to keep a close watch on the men without it being too obvious. Malnutrition was beginning to be felt by all. Even the strongest tired after very little exertion. We were all very thin. There were still scores of men in hospital whose wounds were sometimes as much as eleven months old and were as far as ever from healing. This was the result of the rice diet. The vitamin deficiencies were resulting in the spread of diseases. We visited the hospital every Sunday and each time I went there I became more depressed about the patients' prospects. It was maddening to think that vital medicines were unobtainable, that the Japs had clamped down on the essentials for the hospital. As a contrast, our houses in Quadrant Road had electricity and were a blaze of light at night. You could stroll along and see, through uncurtained windows, men playing bridge or dominoes.

We saw the New Year in with a grand party. John Scrimgeour produced the gramophone and records. A Norfolks officer, Stanley Page (nicknamed 'Pipe'), had a talent for impersonation and provided the highlight. His impression of a Hindu babu nearly had us in hysterics. Looking back, perhaps it wasn't quite so brilliant as it appeared. We were so starved of entertainment that literally anything brought the house down. In the same way even trivial mishaps became a matter of conversational worth. It was becoming harder and harder to find something to talk about.

The monotonous days, with tempers strained by hunger, were a severe test of friendship. But where they survived, such friendships were invaluable. They probably saved many a man's reason. I was lucky in rejoining John and from this point I was to share the rest of the three-and-a-half years of captivity with him.

We never talked about our changed appearance. I remember that at first we talked about escape. This dwindled as time went on and we realized more and more the sheer hopelessness of it. We couldn't be sure where the nearest Allied troops were. Probably Chungking. That would mean a thousand miles through some of the densest jungle in the world. We'd not been trained in jungle survival. And for how long could we successfully disguise ourselves as Malay or Tamil?

Moreover there were ugly rumours reaching us from time to time of men who'd tried to escape being recaptured and promptly sentenced to death by the Japs. We never heard of a successful escape. Gradually even discussion of it as an outside chance dwindled away.

It seemed that our captors could never let us settle down to an organized life. Orders came that we were to move yet again, this time to a sub-area, still in Changi, which became known as the Garden and Wood Area. It was a few miles nearer to Singapore.

I was with the advance party, still in my capacity as officer-in-charge of hygiene. My staff was increased by the addition of a lance-corporal from the Suffolks called Weinstock. In civilian life he turned over large sums of money on the Stock Exchange. I thoroughly enjoyed working with him and it was always a mystery to me that he'd never had a commission.

The Garden and Wood Area was completely undeveloped when we arrived, and our first tasks were to make drains and latrines. There were a few huts in this camp, but quite a number of men had to live under canvas. Sanitation was of prime importance, so I found myself, with the aid of Corporal Matthews and Lance-Corporal Weinstock, in charge of a labour gang. We had to work hard on this not very salubrious but essential job.

One day we were told that we could buy chicks and ducklings, starting our own runs. I became the owner of three alleged hen chicks and a very fierce elderly hen who looked like a game bird, for she actually had purple feathers. She laid a few eggs from time to time. To the amusement of the other poultry farmers my 'hen' chicks started to crow.

One of my many unsavoury jobs was to clear the bore-holes. These were latrines of great depth which we'd dug into the ground by the means of a circular auger. They quickly became infested with blue-bottles and it was vital for our health that these should be destroyed. The method was simple. A gauze cage was placed over the hole. When the lid was suddenly lifted all the flies would swarm up to the light and into the cage. As soon as I had a good supply I singed the cage in a bonfire, killing the wretched creatures and, I hoped, sterilizing them of the dysentery bugs which used them as hosts. The tiny wizened carcasses looked rather like dried black peas. These were a most attractive diet to our feathered pets. I visited the poultry pens, scattering the bluebottle carcasses. I generally sat on a large stone surrounded by a clamouring mob of birds. There were little chicks, ducklings, large hens and cocks, even a few sparrows and other wild birds. My particular favourites were the ducklings. They needed much more attention because they were more delicate and lacked the stamina of the chicks. I used to make sure they had a more than fair share of the bluebottles, and they never failed to come scurrying back for more.

As usual, food was our major problem. Every inch around the hut was devoted to growing vegetables. There was no bartering or buying of food from locals because in the Garden and Wood Area we had no contact with the outside world except permission to cross over to a Dutch area nearby. Here they had a canteen organized and we could get odd luxuries, such as cheroots. We'd have traded all these, though, for food.

Apart from the health hazards resulting from vitamin and other deficiencies, there was the monotony of the daily rice ration which drove us to try anything that might be edible. I decided to start a snail farm. I collected a few healthy specimens, put them in a box of earth and placed them under the hut in the hope they would multiply. They didn't. One day we decided we couldn't wait for them to produce another generation. We'd eat them.

I'd always been fastidious about food, but starvation blunts such niceties. It's true that there was to come a time when, desperately hungry though I was, I would draw the line at the idea of eating dog. But I was prepared to sample the snails.

We'd no very clear idea of how they should be cooked. I boiled them three times in different containers, and at the end of this I considered they looked a little more edible. We then steamed them up and fried them in palm oil. When served they looked not unlike miniature grilled kidneys, but here the resemblance ended. They tasted of nothing in particular. We decided it had hardly been worth the trouble, even though they had added something to the rice.

We all loathed the rice, which never varied in its dull, unappetizing appearance, but so great was our hunger that it was always eaten ravenously.

When I was not occupied with thinking and trying ways of making our diet more tempting I was working hard as hygiene officer. We were getting a number of dysentery cases and suspected there might be more. We issued an order that any man suffering from diarrhoea was to report sick immediately. This was important because it would most probably turn out that the man was going down with dysentery. We suspected, though, that some of the men who were suffering were trying to conceal it, in order to avoid going sick. We had to resort to posting men in the latrines for observation purposes. It wasn't a pleasant job and the results weren't satisfactory. I ultimately had the idea that if we could remove the lowest covering of the screen at the back of the bore-holes we could see the men squatting without having to go inside.

It so happened that very soon after I had instituted this check I had to do my turn at escorting the C.O. of the detachment round the camp. As we passed in the rear of the latrines he suddenly stopped and said, "Burton, do you see the third bottom on the right?"

A bit mechanically I stammered, "Y-yes sir."

"Go round and take its name – it's pouring out pure liquid."

"Very good, Sir!" *Sotto voce*: "The things I do for England."

How successful this health drive would have been I can only guess, because the Japs chose this moment to select another overseas party. Many of my old friends went with this, including John Scrimgeour.

We all believed that they were bound for Japan, just as the other overseas parties had been. We were not to know until afterwards that for the majority Japan was not to be their destination.

No sooner had we started to settle down again than word came that most of the rest of us were to go up-country. As usual there was no definite news. Our Japanese supervisors, if they were aware of our destination, didn't tell us. We were assured that we'd be going to a good camp. And in our foolishness we rather believed this.

While we had till then witnessed very little in the way of atrocities, we had suffered severe privations absolutely contrary to any of the Geneva Conventions. We had realized that prisoners-of-war taken so quickly and in such large numbers had presented the Japs with a major problem. We'd expected, though, that the chaos would sort itself out, that medical supplies would become available, that food would improve. We had some faith in the International Red Cross. After all, prisoners-of-war were their concern. Were they investigating the conditions of our captivity?

Rumour had it that there were Red Cross camps in the Malayan hills, presumably in the Cameron Highlands. Here, it was said, there would be good food, adequate medicines and even some amenities. Some of the promises made by the Japs gave strength to this rumour, but I had secret doubts.

As we were going away it meant that we had to kill the ducks and poultry. This was really distressing. Even though we'd been hungry many times, nobody had suggested that we should make a meal of the birds which had become our pets. They'd added a lot of interest and amusement to our lives. However, after some debate it was decided that this was the only thing to do. We were most unhappy about it. As someone said, "They're so much more human and likeable than the Nips, it seems like murder."

At least the killing was done efficiently. The Norfolks had an oldish man who was expert not only in this but in preparing the carcasses.

With the deed done, our repressed hunger banished remorse. We lived on chicken and duck for the last few days of our stay in the Garden and Wood Area. These were the finest meals I had during the whole of my captivity. We had a surplus of birds and this started a frantic search for jam jars so that we could take ready-cooked food on our journey. We had some British officers from Indian Army regiments and they spared some of their birds for a later date, knocking up a portable hen coop which even had wheels on it.

67

Right to the end we were not able to get any information as to where we were going. I think our local contacts – the warrant officers and N.C.O.s – were as ignorant as we were ourselves. The Japanese chain of command was of a feudal nature. Orders were given, but never any reasons. Immediate obedience was expected and we witnessed several incidents in which officers treated their subordinates like so many cattle.

Apart from preparing our luxury meals and packing cooked birds in jars, we were busily getting ready for our journey. Even in our impoverished state we'd collected some pretty useless belongings. We'd been told to cut down to bare essentials and so the rest had to be thrown away. The best advice was: "Take only what you can carry." Many failed to heed this, only to learn wisdom the hard way.

# Chapter 6

## VALLEY OF THE SHADOW OF DEATH
## APRIL–DECEMBER 1943

We learnt that we were to be called Party H 6, which would be comprised entirely of officers. At our final briefing we knew no more than that we were going up-country by train. We had no inkling that we were going to Siam, as present-day Thailand was then called. It transpired that we were about the last group to go from Singapore. Previous parties had started with the prefix 'A' and numbers 1 to 10. These first parties had established a base camp around Bangkok. Subsequent parties worked farther from this base and railhead.

Unknown to us, the Japanese were suffering heavy shipping losses around the Malay peninsula and so they'd decided to attempt to maintain their army in Burma by rail from Siam. This railway project had been surveyed in peacetime by the Thai government, who'd called in several leading European firms, including experts from Germany. After surveying the ground there had been unanimous rejection of the project. It was regarded as an engineering impossibility owing to the virtually impenetrable jungle, the thickest in the world except for the Amazon basin, and the uneven terrain which would have to be traversed. The cost would be absolutely prohibitive even if the engineers could achieve the impossible.

Perhaps, in addition to the prime military consideration, the Japanese wanted to prove that they could succeed where all others had not even dared to try. In fact we were told this later; the Japanese East Asia Co-prosperity Sphere would build the railway where all had failed. The appalling losses in the prisoner-of-war labour force meant nothing to them.

I think a partial explanation of this lay in the fact that their own troops were supposed to die in combat rather than surrender. There was no idea of reciprocal treatment of prisoners. Any Jap who surrendered deserved whatever might happen to him afterwards – he was no better than a deserter. Undoubtedly we prisoners-of-war were a nuisance, we were in their way. So the best thing was to use us where they could, and it didn't matter if a few thousand died.

So the railway was started. It was the groups under the letters F and H who had to tackle the worst of it. The F Force had to clear the way from railhead to Three Pagoda Pass on the Burma frontier. H Force followed up actually laying the track. We never encountered anyone from G Force, so I imagine they'd been sent elsewhere.

F Force had the most ghastly casualty figures, I think, in the nature of six out of ten, but H Force were not far behind.

We were in happy ignorance of what lay ahead. There was still a hope that the Japs had relented about their treatment of prisoners, perhaps as a result of representations by the Red Cross. Some optimist suggested that as we were an 'officers only' party it must surely mean we were going to a five-star rest camp. I inclined more to the view expressed by others that this was just another of the Jap muddles and we'd probably find ourselves put in charge of Javanese troops.

On the day we marched up to Selerang Barracks from the Garden and Wood Area and paraded on the square we could see the scars across the concrete where, during the 'black hole' episode, men had been forced to dig down to make latrine accommodation. It was a grim reminder. A more cheerful sight was that of transport waiting to take us to Singapore.

Now that we were assembled our H 6 party was about a hundred strong. In command was Major 'Uncle' Evans of the Gurkhas. He was a strong character, as we were to learn in the hideous adversity to come. The party was drawn from the 18th Division – this included John and myself – with the addition of some British officers from the Indian Army, some Australians, and even some Americans.

Among the 18th Division officers were a few I remembered from Serangoon Road, but there was nobody from my original hand-wagon parties. The Indian Army officers were from various regiments including the Gurkhas and some from Mountain Gunners – nicknamed Screw guns. The Americans were Merchant Navy officers from ships which had been torpedoed or sunk by Axis raiders. Their leader, Denis Roland, was a cheerful little man who became a firm friend. He had a ready wit which was invaluable in bad times.

Leaping ahead, I was delighted to renew this friendship when I visited New York in June 1958.

I mention the Australians last, but they were magnificent, and we were most fortunate to have them with us. They were resourceful and highly practical in their approach to living in the jungle. Their back-woodsman type of knowledge was to help us enormously from time to time.

While we were loading up, Eric Prattley, the C.O. of the 5th Norfolks, and the few officers who were, unknowingly at the time, to spend the rest of their captivity in Changi, moved among us to wish us all the best on our journey. They hoped we'd enjoy the trip, that the beds at the hotel would be to our liking, and promised to look us up after the war.

Our transport moved off. Singapore railway station was quite busy, thronged with Orientals. There were not many Jap soldiers, but quite a number of sailors were waiting for trains. They and the civilians seemed interested in us and appeared quite friendly. Everyone was most amused to see the Indian Army officers wheeling their chicken coop full of cackling birds down the platform. Then the Australians were manhandling an upright piano. It was as good as something out of a comedy film. It was all too much for the rising tempers of our Nip guards who started to run around shouting "*Kurrah!*" and boxing the ears of whoever happened to be within reach. This did nothing to subdue us and all our humorists had a grand time at the expense of the Japs, whose pidgin English wasn't good enough to cope with this sort of situation. They couldn't fail to guess that we were laughing at them, which made them all the more infuriated.

However, our amusement died down fast when our train arrived. It was made up of steel box-cars, with sliding doors in the middle of each side. Although these were open, the steel-roofed boxes were like ovens. Our guards proceeded to divide us into parties of thirty, and this involved counting, with the usual Nipponese muddle of re-counting and re-checking. For a master race their educational standard was very low, and the counting of thirty men almost beyond them. The result was more rage and ear-boxing all round. They seemed to get mad at each other.

Thirty officers and all their luggage were allocated to each steel box. The luggage was put in first, then we followed, our guards shoving at us, hitting us, or pricking us with their bayonets. In some

71

amazing way the full thirty managed to clamber into the box. We had to sit as well as we could on the luggage, and there was only sufficient room to sit bolt upright. The only way to stretch one's legs was to stand up, balanced precariously on the luggage. We kept a small clear space near the open doors so that anyone in need of a stretch and some fresh air could stand there. There was a solitary chain across and it was necessary to hold this because of the train's jolting.

We were off to a jolting start almost without warning and we were soon going over the causeway into Johore. This was only the second time I'd crossed. Previously I'd been on a lorry from Havelock Road which was to pick up pineapples at Kota Tinggi. That time I'd not had a good look at the causeway, but this time, thanks to the open doors, I could see that it had been breached on the Johore side, though the Japs had accomplished makeshift repairs. This breaching had been done on the eve of the battle for Singapore and there was now some lively discussion between us about the tactics of this. I was sure we should have done the breaching on the island side so that the gap would have been within range of our small arms fire. I didn't need to be a Staff College graduate to make this erudite observation.

When we grew tired of discussion John and I opened a jam jar containing what he described as "Chicken à la Aspic de Changi" and we enjoyed this while jolting and swaying on our way north up the Malay peninsula.

Towards evening it grew chilly. John had an old tweed jacket and he put this on. At one wayside halt a kindly-meant remark from a Jap guard raised roars of laughter. He came down the train counting the prisoners and said to John, "Why you wear wool coat, are you sick?"

John answered immediately, "Yes – sick of this bloody journey." The Jap said, "Ah – so. No good-eega," and gave him two creosote pills.

It was dark when we reached Kuala Lumpur. Here the train stopped and the guards started to shout, "Orume (all men) go Benjo." There was a tremendous scramble across the platform to the Gents which resulted in a queue forming. Some enterprising officers decided to waive sex distinctions and invaded the Ladies to the consternation of some very flustered elderly Malay women. They came running out shrieking. The Jap guards were amused and laughed.

When the lavatory procedure was over we queued again for a wad of wet rice and a mug of black tea. Then we returned to our steel boxes. It had been wonderful to stretch our legs, but they quickly stiffened again. Night proved worse than day. It was difficult to sleep sitting up. If you toppled over or kicked out in your sleep some other unfortunate suffered. There was a tantalizing clear space near the open doors, but it wasn't safe to sleep there in case you rolled out under the chain.

So sleep came only in snatches and by morning we were still tired and very cramped. And the miserably uncomfortable journey showed no promise of ending. That we were bound for some paradise of a rest camp was becoming less and less likely.

Experiencing these cramped, overheated conditions, I wondered how those officers had fared who had to take a mixed crowd of troops on journeys such as this. How had they managed to keep up morale, and how much self-sacrifice had there been in the way of taking lashings from the Jap guards because of trying to insist on the men's rights?

In retrospect, bad as things were to become, they would have been far worse but for the spirit of endurance which H 6 party seemed to possess. It must have been one of the finest Allied efforts of the war when one considers the frictions and irritations which can arise when conditions are so bad. One can recognize the value of comradeship, but it's a very different matter to practise it when it means a little more effort at the very moment you're so weary you just want to die in peace. Throughout the nightmare to come we had no major quarrels amongst ourselves.

We were to be fortunate in another way. The necessary discipline for survival was understood and accepted by everybody. It didn't have to be imposed. To give a positive example, nobody broke the injunction to drink only water that had been boiled. The result was that, throughout, H 6 party didn't have a single cholera case. With even well-disciplined troops there would have been a few who regarded such instructions as "a perfect bloody nuisance" and taken a chance. The cholera figures proved it.

Returning to our rail journey northwards, this seemed to go on for ever. It became obvious that we were not bound for so pleasant a spot as Frazer's Hill, or the Cameron Highlands. Our sense of time went. I think our journey lasted some five days and four nights – though it seemed very much longer. I began to fear that I would lose the use of my legs, cramp seeming to have twisted them up internally. It became more and more difficult to stand on the luggage and maintain balance. We were all in a heavy-eyed condition through lack of restful sleep and the conditions were particularly bad for those suffering from dysentery. They had to hold on to the chain and relieve themselves through the open doors.

We had a bad time when the train stopped and the Jap guards came along and closed all the doors. We wondered if it was some new form of inhumanity as the hours passed and the heat and airlessness increased. However, the door-closing was merely a security measure. We'd passed through Alor Star which was now a large Jap airfield. Why they should have troubled themselves about what we might see I don't know; perhaps it was just an example of their obsession with secrecy for secrecy's sake.

At last, mercifully, we reached our destination, which was Bampong on the outskirts of Bangkok. The last stage of the journey had aroused our interest. We'd looked out on the rice fields of Siam and seen the ploughing being done by elephants, and this sight had fascinated us. It had a children's story-book quality, and this was enhanced by the labouring coolies who wore enormous hats like flat plates. At the small stations we had a closer look at the Thais, for they swarmed round the train, selling fruit for old clothes. All this confusion angered the Jap guards, who resorted to their usual ear-boxing tactics. The Thai railway officials remained rather aloof from this. They reminded me of so many brigadiers with the red bands around their hats.

At the end of the journey we struggled to unload all the gear which had provided such uncomfortable seating. The platform became more and more littered with luggage. Looking back along the train I saw the Australians manhandling the upright piano. I wondered if they'd enlivened the monotony of the journey by a sing-song marathon. But this was the end of the road for the piano. My last sight of it was where it stood in solitary grandeur just outside the left luggage office. I often wonder what became of it. I doubt if it would have survived the climate for long.

We lined up and marched down the road. It was splendid to be able to move our legs freely, and the march was not so long that it exhausted us, though at the end of a mile the gear we were carrying had become very heavy and decidedly hard and uncomfortable. As we reached what was supposed to be a staging camp the rain started to fall. It was real tropical rainfall, and not the first storm of the day as the state of the ground bore witness.

I've seen few places more depressing. There was a literal sea of mud and, arising from this, in the centre of the clearing, was a solitary big hut. I think the Jap guards were almost as depressed as we were. They certainly seemed anxious to explain that this was only a staging camp and to promise "New campo very goodeega. You go asta (tomorrow)," but the good new camp was very much like tomorrow; it never came!

We splashed through the quagmire and reached the hut. It was almost as muddy within as it was outside. We squelched around, trying to arrange our belongings so that they remained as dry as possible and this was exceedingly difficult because the roof of the hut seemed to leak in a thousand places. So we spent a night almost as uncomfortable as those in the train, where we had at least been dry. As an introduction to Siam I felt this was about as grim as it could be.

With the morning sunshine we all felt a bit brighter. We tried to dry our soaked garments and, in spite of the squalor of the camp, there was a certain feeling of freedom, for there was no perimeter wire. Our guards made some show of posting sentries, but circumstances were rather too much for them when the Thai villagers descended on us. There was some brisk trading. They offered boiled eggs and bananas for old clothes. The general bustle and confusion of the trading gave opportunities to the dishonest. The most unlucky victim was an officer who had to go to the latrines and had his trousers stolen, virtually from under his nose.

We had been warned that we would do our marching by night, resting during the day. The Japs also said we would have to march for only two nights. This might be so, but we never believed them until promises were borne out by events.

At ten o'clock in the evening we lined up, laden with our gear, and marched away from the hut in the sea of mud. I noticed that the crate of cackling hens was no longer with us. I imagined they had been traded and were now in the possession of some Thai villager.

Marching into the darkness, our spirits were reasonably high at first. Some wag suggested we should detail a party to go back to Bampong for the piano. But after a time the cheerfulness wore off. Just how much to carry was a really difficult problem. With comparatively few possessions each became more precious and there was always the thought that starvation might be kept at bay a little longer by trading some article or other for food. The result was that some of the officers were desperately overloaded, so that the march became a very stiff ordeal. It was strange that after a certain distance the most carefully packed burden became so very uncomfortable.

"My stuff's changed into granite chips," someone complained.

Another officer expressed the strong belief that his bedding roll had turned into a marble plinth.

It was a long march in the darkness. The man in front of me had a white bowl strapped on his back. It served as a marking disc. I was almost hypnotized by that white blob as it bobbed up and down and swayed a little from side to side. Sometimes I could see nothing else and I followed it mechanically. I had good reason to remember this particular event, since the man in front was my good friend Peter Playfair, a young Australian officer with whom I developed a close bond, lasting throughout our captivity until I saw him off at the end of the war. He returned to Australia on the troopship *Duntroon*. Sadly, when many years later I tried to look him up in Sydney, I was told that he had been very badly injured in a traffic accident and could not communicate. I was advised not to see him, but I will always remember how he had helped me on that march all those years ago in Thailand.

With brief rests we marched all through the night and at dawn we reached some stilted buildings which terraced the open slope down to a fairly large river. I never discovered the name of this place. We were told we could fall out and rest and we more or less dropped down where we stood. We were so tired that we spent the first part of the morning stretched out on the ground asleep. But as noon came nearer the heat increased and the sun's brightness was torment, and so we moved into the shade under the platforms of the huts.

We were given our usual ration of boiled rice, but once more the Thai villagers were among us, eager to trade. Taking a closer look I could see that in the midst of the other houses of the village there was one which was quite large. This, we found, was occupied by Buddhist priests. They came to see us and their saffron robes gave a bright touch of colour to the scene. The priests appeared to be as interested in trading as the villagers were, but their requirements were different. They moved among us saying, "Parker-pen, Parker-pen." I don't think any of us had a possession of such value.

The farmers and small traders from the village were mostly in blue with the curious plate hats we'd already seen. The women wore white blouses with blue skirts, though some were in trousers. They were in the majority and it seemed they did all the work, for they carried the wares on yokes slung across their shoulders. From one end a charcoal brazier dangled – alight. A large metal bowl hung from the other end.

When the bartering was done and the meal ordered, each woman produced a small stool, squatted, placed the large metal bowl on the brazier and proceeded to 'fry up' rice, eggs, bamboo shoots, and other ingredients. The result, which they called *Mah Mee*, and which translated means 'friend mixture', was delicious.

The afternoon was spent bathing in the river and it was sheer luxury to immerse our hot, dusty bodies in cool running water. We found it almost miraculously refreshing. Our bathing was watched by the interested villagers. Again there were opportunities for pilferers and one officer returned from a swim only just in time to recover his shorts from a Thai who was about to make off with them. Although we had so many spectators, of both sexes, we didn't feel embarrassed.

The Jap guards did nothing to prevent our trading and made no attempt to interfere with the villagers. Although we were in ignorance of the situation, the Thais were technically allies of Japan, since they had signed a treaty on the eve of invasion. There was a long tradition of friendship between Britain and Siam, but perhaps the Thais couldn't be blamed for severing this so abruptly. They'd had ample proof, from the tragedy in Malaya, that we were in no position to defend them and they were certainly in no position to defend themselves against so efficient a fighting force as the Japanese army. The Thais showed no hostility to us at any time, and we had the impression they had little love for their Japanese allies. Certainly the Japs bullied them, and on later occasions broke up their efforts to trade with us. Perhaps the forbearance of our guards this time was due to the fact that they recognized we would be in better shape for continuing the long march if we had eaten well.

As evening drew near we were warned that we would soon be on the move again. The Thai traders were ready and we enjoyed a hearty meal of *Mah Mee*. We were blissfully ignorant that this would be about the last decent meal we were to get for many long months to come.

Soon after this meal we were ordered to line up ready for resuming our march. There was the inevitable confusion over counting us, involving numbering and re-numbering, and it seemed part of the ritual that some faces should be slapped. When this was over we set off and our spirits were higher because our sore feet had been soothed a bit and freshened, and for once our stomachs felt full.

The going was hard, though, and although we'd all packed our meagre but precious belongings as carefully as possible they were uncomfortable burdens. In point of fact, this second night march saw quite a number of our prized possessions cast away into the darkness. Any weight on our ill-padded and weary backs was well-nigh intolerable. Even so, there were willing hands to help the weakest and the most exhausted. I felt that comradeship couldn't go to much greater lengths than this. Even those who took on extra burdens were physically in no condition to make the march.

Each one of us suffered his own personal agony, though it was generally hidden by cheerfulness of a macabre nature. An officer of the Indian Army who was near to me removed his boots and tied them round his neck, marching over the far from soft ground in stockinged feet. Anything, he told me, was preferable to the torturing rubbing and chafing of lacerated flesh against leather.

So we pressed on into the night. We were on a properly made road, approximately equivalent to a third-class one in England. A bus service ran along it, and indeed the Japs commandeered this transport towards dawn in order to bring in the stragglers.

The pace of our march gradually slowed down. The stops became more and more frequent. Our eyes eventually became accustomed to the dark and I was able to observe that we were crossing a plain and making for a high range of mountains. Against the skyline the crags looked formidable. I prayed that there would be no climbing for us; it would be physically impossible.

Our Jap guards were not too hard on us and it seemed to me that some of them were as eager to rest as any of us. But there was some bad treatment. After we'd been on the march for about a couple of hours some of the physically weaker officers dropped out. The orderly column began to break. Luckily I was able to keep on plodding, but I could hear the angry shouts of the guards as they tried to round up these stragglers. In the darkness the staccato shouts seemed more animal than they did by day. An Australian remarked that you'd only to listen to realize that the Nips were closely related to monkeys. There were other sounds, infuriating not amusing, as the Japs lost their tempers and started to beat the offenders.

Officially we tried to keep to the marching routine of the British Army, a ten-minute rest every hour. Whenever we stopped we flung ourselves on the ground without bothering to free ourselves of the packs we were carrying. That would have wasted precious resting time and for my part, at least, there would have been the devil's own job getting the stuff on my back once more. It seemed to be all straps and fixtures.

Starting up again was absolute torture. Every muscle in the body seemed to protest with agonizing twinges. Somehow I managed to totter to the road and stagger on. The others were faring no better. There were no longer any jokes. We pressed on in grim silence in a sort of mental stupor. I couldn't think clearly. I had to concentrate on getting one foot ahead of the other, then moving the first one again . . . and keeping it up. We passed through villages but I scarcely noticed them.

I couldn't really think about the others because my own personal struggle was so great. Somehow, after each rest, I joined them, or those of them who were still staggering along in what now seemed a death march. There were some who just lay where they'd dropped, insensible to the shouts, the sickening thumps with rifle butts, the kickings, and the proddings with bayonets. At length even the Japs gave up, and so our worst cases were eventually picked up and brought on by bus.

But for me the nightmare persisted. We'd started out marching three abreast; we finished in a straggling, wavering, single file. There were great distances between us and the Japs tried to close these up. They had already warned us that Thai bandits would be stealing up in our rear ready to pick off stragglers, whom they'd murder and rob of every stitch they possessed. This may have been a story invented to keep us going, or it could have been perfectly true. The Japs gave the impression of being rather scared, and some of the men at the rear of our column said afterwards that they were sure they'd seen figures slinking around and following them up. However, if there were bandits, they didn't attack.

With dawn our exhaustion and misery became more and more obvious. The men ahead of me were swaying down the centre of the road as if blind. It was a mystery to me why I didn't fall. I must have been walking as if drugged.

Unexpectedly we saw the tall chimney of a factory. The Japs pointed to this and exclaimed, "Campo – very goodega." There would, they promised us, be food and rest.

This place we were approaching was Kanchanaburi (or Kanburi).

But before we reached it the familiar Thai traders appeared. I don't know whether they'd been forewarned or whether they could sense that we were approaching. They turned and moved alongside, some with small carts, others with yokes slung across their shoulders. The Japs made only a token show of driving them off, and so we were able to obtain the meagre refreshment they had to offer.

We were pretty impoverished, especially as stuff had been thrown away during the long night march. The few coins and some tattered garments seemed to satisfy the traders. Perhaps they were being kind to us.

An ample-bosomed Thai woman trotted alongside me dispensing bowls of sweetened coffee. I had it black and was glad afterwards when one of the other officers vowed he'd seen her providing the milk from her breasts.

We had a half-hour halt in a small village at just about dawn and this helped us to complete our straggling journey. These last-minute refreshments from the Thais had a wonderful effect. We were able to produce a feeble imitation of a swinging march.

The sun was up as we halted in an open space near some huts. We'd reached Kanchanaburi and, it seemed, the last flicker of our endurance. We collapsed. There was no crawling to shade, no easing of the abominable burdens of our packs. Men went to sleep as they crumpled to the ground. It was so with me. The next thing I knew was awakening with all my equipment strapped and tied round my body and the sun blazing overhead. I was less exhausted but I felt terrible. John was in a similar plight, though he must have had a harder time than I because he still walked with a limp.

As I blinked at the brightness and struggled painfully back to consciousness I was astonished to see Donald Wise standing over me. He'd been carrier officer in the 4th Suffolks and had come up to Kanchanaburi with F Force. He bullied and persuaded me to move into the shade. Some of the others joined us. Wise had been with F Force but he'd fallen sick and they had left him behind. He'd been in this place for some time and was able to answer some of our eager questions.

From what he was able to tell us, all the indications pointed to our being in for a rough time.

We must have presented a strange sight as we talked. We were all emaciated and in tattered uniforms. Overhead was the blazing sun. There were shrubs and bushes giving small patches of shade and there were a few atap huts. This might, I thought, be the end of the world. Perhaps it was; we were certainly on the threshold of Purgatory.

Donald Wise was the opposite number to the carrier officer of the Norfolks who'd been savagely decapitated during the battle, and I'd not seen him since Changi. He, of course, had left well ahead of us with F Force. His illness and having to be left behind had probably saved his life. Of course, he looked near death, worse than at Changi. But this was true of all of us and we never mentioned or discussed it.

Donald was able to tell us of a steady stream of prisoners of all nationalities. Not all were military; there were large parties of civilian coolies. Rumours had filtered back of the inhuman drive to construct the railway, of the slave-like gangs, the cruelly enforced marches, the death camps. You could be going into some of these, we heard, and there were those which had been left for the dead and dying.

I think all of us had cherished the foolish belief that Kanchanaburi was our final destination. We were bitterly disillusioned. To me the future bore so nightmarish an aspect that my brain refused to accept it. But uncomfortable reason told me that it was all too possible. We were in the hands of virtual savages – for we'd seen that the civilization of these people was just a thin veneer – they were completely indifferent as to our fate. This was not the premeditated, coldly worked out brutality of the Germans. Japanese brutality was a thing of the moment, born of a savagery of temper. The man who beat you up one day was quite capable of offering you a smoke the next. Indeed something very similar happened to our own stragglers from the night march. They joined us towards lunchtime. The Japs had commandeered the local bus and brought them along in it. Last night these guards had kicked, bludgeoned and bayonet-jabbed their near-insensible prisoners. But on the bus journey they distributed a few cheroots.

Whatever ordeals and torments lay ahead, we were for the moment left in peace. We made ourselves as comfortable as we could in the shade of the bushes. We bathed our feet from our mess-tins or water-bottles. We talked a little and we slept a lot.

By evening all the stragglers had been rounded up and our numbers were complete again. We were told that the next day we would continue our journey by train. This night we were to spend where we were – out in the open.

I slept near to John. We'd unrolled our blankets under a bush. Towards dawn it started to drizzle. Still drowsy and cursing under our breath, we managed to interlace our groundsheets and crawled under them. As a makeshift tent it was a rather dismal failure. Our companions fared no better. When day came we were all more or less soaked to the skin.

During the morning a few Australians appeared. It seemed they were drivers. Their manner was quite furtive as they sought out the Australian officers in our party and talked with them. We learnt afterwards what they'd had to say and some of it was shockingly grim.

There were Allied prisoners in the atap huts which we could see from our open space camp. But orders were strict that there was to be no communication. It wasn't until we knew this that we realized what a risk Donald Wise had taken in coming over to us. Most of what he'd told us was confirmed by the Australians.

They'd told one grim and blood-chilling story of how, over in a nearby hut, the prisoners, six in number, had somehow managed to assemble a wireless set. The Jap guards caught them operating it and the six prisoners-of-war were marched out and beheaded.

In all this bad news there was one glimmer of hope. The Aussie drivers had said that the Jap campaign in Burma was going badly. Most of the shipping coming round the Malay peninsula to supply their army in Burma was being sunk. Yet there was a bad side to this, for in desperation the Japs were flinging everything into getting the railway built. Every prisoner who could stand was being forced to work.

It was a bad prospect, but we agreed with the Australian who said, "I'll put up with some extra hardship if it means the Nip bastards are copping a packet."

All the discussion, which this fresh news had started was brought to an end by the Japs, who started to parade us in readiness for moving on. As we began to march from the open space I think we all suspected that the story about going by train was just another lie.

However, we were marched to a railway line where there was a train made up of open trucks. This was far from first-class accommodation, but most of us knew from experience how much better these would be than the metal boxes in which we'd travelled up from Singapore.

As we boarded the trucks we were very cheerful. Of course, at the back of our minds there was the drilled-in knowledge that survival hinged on making the best of things, and so we clutched at any straw. Our misery – for we were all undernourished, terribly underweight,

1. The inner perimeter of Changi gaol.


2. Changi gaol seen from the Coolie Lines.

3. Changi gaol seen from the main road.

4. Changi gaol from the air.

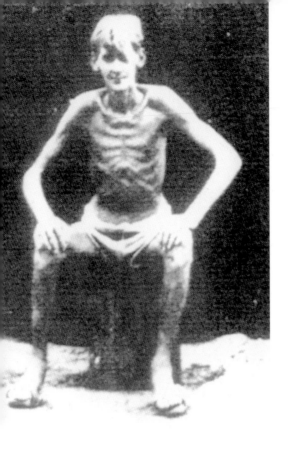

5. Passed fit for work on the railway

6. Railway sleepers cut from teak tree trunks. *(Sears Eldredge)*

7. Hintok Cutting. Hewn by hand out of solid rock by POWs. *(Sears Eldredge*

(a) entrance

(b) exit

8. An American's idea of an Englishman's impression of an American gangster play.

AMERICAN'S IDEA OF AN ENGLISHMAN'S IMPRESSION OF AN AM...

# GANGSTER PLAY

Cast ———→

ORDER OF APPEARANCE.

ANDY ... a barman ... JOE MANELLA
TONY ... a waiter .... GERRY LE VINE
'FINGERS' BODINSKI .. big shot .. LLOYD JENSEN
CHOPPER' O'SHEA ⎫                ⎧ DON SMITH
TONY LIGORY      ⎬ bodinski's  ⎨ DENIS ROLAND
COKEY JOE        ⎭ mobsters     ⎩ GRAHAM SAUVAGE
NICK DETOLIO ... rival bigshot ... STANLEY WILMER
PAULA DONOGHUE ... singer ... WILLIE SMITH
POLICEMAN ... ... ... MICK MURPHY
SUSY ANDEWS ... a moll ... CHARLES DOLMAN
TUXEDO JIM CASSIDY ...
            new trigger man .. OWEN BAGGETT
BUTCH MALONE .. detolio mobster  ALF MEN?
        PIANIST
## BILL WILLIAMS ♩♫

☆ Play by BURTON AND FOWLER

☆ Produced by JAMIESON AND BURTON

STAGE MANAGER. JOHN HAYNE
ASSISTANT S.M . MICK BURGESS

9. Cast of *Speakeasy* by Ronald Searle.

10. The surrender of the Japanese in Singapore. *(IWM)*

11. The Japanese arrive at Singapore Town Hall. *(IWM)*

12. The arrival of General Saito, C-in-C Malaya. *(IWM)*

13. One month after our release. Author on the left, John Hayne on the right.

suffering from some skin disease or other ailment – was such that we were thankful for any improvement in our condition. I found for myself – and I believe it was true for many others – that I'd no great awareness of the future. Perhaps it was a form of self-protection. The prospect ahead, a captivity of unknown length with protracted ordeals we'd experienced all too many times, could easily have built up a suicidal state of mind. The safe way was to live for the moment and not look ahead. Tomorrow we might be marching again and I might be one of the victims who'd die on the way, but for the moment I could rest my legs and I was in a train.

We began to pass railway camps full of Allied soldiers, who waved and shouted greetings to us. They were very similar in appearance, these isolated shanty towns. There were improvised wooden huts, old tents, and some canvas awnings. Most of them had a bamboo stockade as the perimeter, a constant reminder that they were prisoner-of-war camps.

We crossed a large river by means of a modern steel bridge. And nearby was a bigger camp, the capital of the shanty towns. It was called Tamarkand Bridge Camp and I was to get to know it quite well. There were rows of large, well-built huts. Gravel paths led to the cook-houses and the latrines. There were roads too, while at the lesser camps there were only paths which became canals of mud after every heavy tropical storm.

My hope that we might have been unloaded at this more attractive camp was a vain one. The train chugged painfully on, swaying and lurching perilously on the tracks as we started the long climb alongside a ravine. It was frightening to look out. On the one hand there was a sheer cliff rising above us and on the other a long drop to a foaming yellowish-brown river.

We were in denser jungle, too, so that it seemed we were being taken farther and farther away from civilization. After turning a few bends we had a distant view forward of what I learnt afterwards was Wampo Viaduct. It was so far away it looked like a toy constructed from interlaced matchsticks. But as we drew nearer, the matchsticks increased and increased in size until we could see they were enormous logs. Like Tamarkand, this bridge was over a ravine. Later, when we reached Tarsao, some Australians who came down to visit their fellow officers in our H 6 Force told how this bridge had been built by Australian slave labour and that several of the men had been brutally murdered by the Japs in charge of them. They'd been beaten with sticks so that they'd toppled off and crashed down into the ravine.

"The Nips up here are ripe bloody swine," we were warned.

But at this time we knew nothing of the bridge's evil history. Although the logs were so enormous, the construction looked terribly flimsy when you bore in mind the weight of the heavy train. I think we all held our breath and felt great relief when we reached the other side. I know I had the feeling that I daren't look out.

I was destined to make a return journey through this country, though I was to know nothing of it because I'd be in the throes of delirium induced by incessant bouts of malaria culminating in black-water fever.

Many of us travelling up, though, were in no fit condition. There was one poor fellow suffering badly from dysentery. He provided us with our best laugh of the day. He had to be helped to the side of the open wagon and held while he relieved himself. This was happening while the train slowed down to go through a wayside station. A Japanese officer stood watching, at attention, his Samurai sword in evidence, his uniform spotless, his jackboots highly polished. At least, the boots were highly polished until the wagon with the dysentery sufferer trundled past. The mishap was spotted at once by at least half the men in the train and the roars of laughter would certainly have resulted in severe beatings had the train not continued on its way. The Jap officer, mad with rage, grabbed for a stone and threw it with cricket-ground accuracy at the offending backside, so that there was an anguished howl from the dysentery patient.

Shortly after this incident we ground to a halt at the railhead. This was Tarsao.

It was here that dense jungle started. On the night march from Bampong to Kanburi we had traversed the plain. The country was flat, with scrub, and near the villages there were paddy fields. Since our train journey started we'd been ascending the valley of the Kwai-Nam-Kong River, climbing higher and coming into jungle which grew thicker and thicker.

Tarsao railhead was a sort of jungle-railway Crewe, with a number of sidings and several engines and trucks. The camp itself was no more than a collection of huts. But before we could reach it we, the new slaves, were officially handed over to our new masters. I looked at the brutish faces of the Japanese soldiers and the equally ugly N.C.O. in charge of them.

"They're an evil-looking bunch," I said out of the side of my mouth to my neighbour.

There was a quick proof of their evil tempers. A major of the Suffolks, a very sick man, was a bit slow in climbing down from the wagon. The Jap N.C.O. turned on him and felled him with a swinging blow to the head with a rifle butt. I thought he was dead and the sheer bestial cruelty made me feel sick. However, the victim managed to get to his feet and totter into line.

When we were lined up the insane counting, re-counting, and checking took place according to the now familiar routine.

One of the Australians said, "A pack of flaming apes couldn't make a bigger muddle of it."

The incident involving the sick major had a profound effect on us all. We'd met, and suffered, brutality before – but this had come so suddenly that it was like the tearing aside of a veil. Despite their efficiency in war, their Western-type uniforms and their modern and mechanized equipment, the Japanese were always quick to revert to barbaric savagery. We'd have fared little worse, probably much better, if we'd fallen into the hands of some primitive race.

My thoughts were very troubled. I wondered how long we could endure the brutalities and the degradation of our filthy and unsanitary surroundings. However weak we became physically, it was clear our captors would show us little or no mercy. It was a quality unknown to the majority of them.

Once we were lined up we left the railhead, passing the engines of the Siamese railway, which were wood-burning. The track was just a ribbon cut through the jungle. Through the dense foliage we had occasional glimpses of high crags. These were the mountain ridges of the Kwai-Nam-Kong valley. We also had the occasional sight of the river far below us. It was muddy but less sluggish than at the place between Bampong and Kanburi where we'd bathed. We were to discover that it became more of a torrent when it rained. It appeared to be navigable though, because there was barge traffic between Tarsao and Tonchan. I believe some craft went even farther up-river.

We marched along this jungle track for a short distance and were then granted a rest. We flung ourselves down on each side of the track. Among the trees there was a collection of huts, clear indication that a camp had been set up. I was surprised to discover, a bit later, that it had been established by men of my own battalion – the 4th Royal Norfolks. I learnt this when we were visited by Colonel

85

Knights, my C.O.; it cheered me up enormously to meet him again. He was now the Senior British Officer in Tarsao and this, Tarsao being the railhead, was a very important job. He had some of his own officers and men with him. I heard that he had done extremely well in a most difficult position, giving all the assistance possible to those who were fortunate enough to be with him.

He and his original party had come up in advance of the ill-fated F Force and they'd established as good a camp as possible. He did his best to cheer us up and to encourage us. He didn't tell us just how grim the future would be, and in this I think he was wise. There was nothing to be gained by spreading gloom and lowering what spirit we still possessed.

At first we hoped we were going to be retained at the railhead, but it was not to be. When night came we were on the march once more. There was frequent rainfall, though we were sheltered to a certain extent by the jungle. The rain seemed to bring out the unpleasant smell of rotting vegetation. It was so dark that we could see very little, but I had the feeling of being hemmed in. This was my first experience of dense jungle and, miserable as our circumstances were, I was thankful not to be alone. There was none of the friendliness of English woods. Here it was all strangely threatening. Perhaps this had something to do with the extraordinary vigour of the vegetable life, with everything growing feverishly in an endeavour to reach up to the light. I suppose there were many wild creatures. It was easy to imagine that countless pairs of eyes were watching from the thick security of the undergrowth. After this experience I've never felt superior when I've read of primitive tribes who believe the jungle to be the realm of powerful spirits who demand propitiation. Had I been alone I'd probably have come to believe something similar myself.

We were moving along a cart-track full of deep ruts. It was difficult to keep to our feet. We slithered and often fell nearly waist-deep into stinking jungle mud. The exertion and the lack of any currents of fresh air along the enclosed track made the sweat pour from us. Although the sky must have cleared after the rain, we could see no stars when we looked up from our jungle ravine.

I had John at my side. I was carrying his 'weekend' bag and giving him what support I could with my other arm. His ankle was still bad and he found the going very hard. He was floundering all over the place.

There were many slimy potholes along the track and we supported each other over the worst patches by linking hands. Whenever anyone fell, the rest halted until the unfortunate could be hauled up on his feet again. This happened frequently and the continuous delays angered our Jap guards. They, too, were feeling the strain and we were entertained by a story passed along the line. One Jap was so weary and staggering that an Australian near to him said, "You're dead beat, sport. Shall I carry your gun for you?" The humorist was known to us all as Bert Savile and he was a wonderful character, a real old-timer. He was one of the group who'd managed to bring along the piano for quite a distance. He was a man of many parts and in many ways made our lot a little easier to bear, especially later on when he was in charge of the cook-house.

After several hours of this gruelling march we were halted and the Japs came along the column shouting, "All men stopka. Yasumé (rest) Campo very goodega."

But there was no camp here, only a soddened clearing in the jungle. The ground was soft and muddy, but we were too far gone to notice. We flopped down and sleep relieved our aching bodies.

When I awoke it was morning. John was up and about kneeling at my side, offering me a cup of hot, sweet tea. It was unbelievable, but tea had been supplied to every member of H 6 by another British party (a gunner camp) nearby.

At daybreak there was yet another unpleasant surprise for us. This very clearing in the jungle, we were told, was our new home – our camp at Tonchan South. Although we couldn't see them, there were several other camps in the vicinity. There was a stream just beyond our site, and on the other side of this were the comparatively luxurious quarters of the Japanese engineers. They had well-built huts, good quality tents and all the amenities, including beds and raffia matting. These engineers, incidentally, wore Imperial Japanese Army uniform and were waited on by Korean orderlies and servants. The Koreans were given all the dirty work and their obsequious fawning certainly earned no reward in the way of kindly treatment.

We had Korean guards. On average they were taller and lighter skinned than their Japanese masters. They had poorer uniform and equipment. Their rifles were mostly captured Allied weapons, with British .303 rifles predominating. In their behaviour to us they displayed more cruelty than the Japs, probably with the idea of winning favour.

But to return to the camps. Above us there was a large one crowded with Tamils, while between us and the river there was the Gunner camp. The men here were engaged in laying lines for communications.

It was a strange feeling to have so many fellow-prisoners near to us and yet so rarely to see them and to have no contact with them. At night we could hear the poor Tamils chattering away to each other. After a few nights we regarded this as one of the normal nocturnal noises.

We spent our first day settling in. There was nothing provided so we had to use all our ingenuity and a lot of our precious strength in making the necessary shelters. It was very necessary to have adequate cover, for this was the south-west monsoon period, the hot, rainy season. This lasts from April to October, when it is followed by the dry north-east monsoon period during which there is a comparatively cool spell in December and January.

There wasn't very much we could do on this first day except to make lean-tos out of the trees under the skilled direction of the Australians, who were exceedingly handy at such tasks. The fact that we ever constructed a camp at all was amazing, because from then on we were paraded before dawn and marched out to work along the track, and we were not brought back until after dark. The work was gruelling and even the fittest among us had very little strength left when we were back in camp. However, somehow the miracle was achieved. We made a cookhouse, latrines and a medical hut. Because of the constant rain and the prevailing mud, duckboards were a necessity; we made them from bamboo.

Somehow we managed to patch up bits and pieces and erect canvas tents. My own particular party numbered sixteen, and we at last found shelter under the outer covering of what was officially known as a European Personnel Indian Pattern tent. It was designed to hold eight men, so we were badly crowded. Quite close to us some of the others had pitched a ragged old bell tent which was like Buckingham Palace compared with the others.

The general appearance of the place was not far removed, I imagined, from a shanty village in the old wild west. But perhaps those didn't have duckboards.

Bert Savile, generally known as Old Bert, was a provost officer and he became the organizer of the cookhouse. He was a First World War soldier with tremendous stamina for his age. His fellow Australian helpers in the cookhouse were John Norbury, a lieutenant in the infantry, and Spike Grieve, also an infantry officer. Poor Spike was going bald and this was the subject of many jokes. For some reason he was nicknamed Snipe. He was always protesting about this, saying plaintively, "Turn it up! You know my name's Spike!"

Our daily task was to press along the lane cut through virgin jungle by the ill-fated F Force and complete the levelling of the ground in readiness for the laying of the track. This meant cutting away stumps and roots left after the rough clearing. It was sometimes necessary for us to fell more trees. The trunks of these and of the trees felled by F Force had to be taken back for sawing.

We always returned at the day's end in the last stages of exhaustion. One such evening we were called upon to make a further effort – in the interests of our camp this time. We needed bamboo for bed-making. So several of us set off to gather some. Suddenly an enormous snake slithered out of a bamboo clump. It made straight for the camp with the working party in pursuit. The creature disappeared into a tent occupied by men who were trying to go to sleep and such was their lethargy that they refused to move. Some of them said quite frankly that they'd risk snake-bite in preference to turning out and searching for the reptile. And there was the inevitable doubter who said sleepily, "I don't believe you've seen a bloody snake at all."

Bert, the old-timer, vowed that snakes often came into the cookhouse at night, seeking the warmth behind the fire chamber. I never saw one myself, so this may have been one of his stories.

Of course the jungle around us was alive with wild creatures, most of whom gave voice at night. There seemed to be no escaping from the saw-mill. We heard it cutting the teak into lengths for sleepers during the day; by night there was a jungle cricket which made an astonishingly similar sound to that of a revolving saw blade cutting into wood. There must have been thousands of these crickets, judging by the sound volume, which suggested that the saw-mill was working overtime. In addition to these there was a full insect orchestra making every possible strident and vibrating noise. Quite startling, if the animals were near, was the whooping of the monkeys.

There were sometimes more threatening noises and several of us quite believed there must be the odd tiger around. We were told, though, that mostly we were hearing hyenas, jackals and wild dogs.

These dogs were a terrible scourge, because nearly all of them were infected with rabies, and they frequently came scavenging around the cookhouse at night. I saw one of these miserable creatures in the light from the cookhouse fire and he was both a pathetic and sickening sight, for half his flank was raw of fur and his entrails were bulging out of a gaping wound.

There was one rabid wild dog which met a merciful end when a good shot among us managed to borrow a rifle from the Japs on the grounds that it was necessary to kill the dog before he bit anyone; the British prisoner was a better shot than any of the Japs and consequently there wouldn't be any waste of ammunition. Surprisingly, perhaps, our captors went along with this.

Most of the night noises were disturbing, but it always seemed to me that one of the worst things about the jungle had nothing to do with noise. It was the smell. With heavy rainfall and the day temperatures rising up to the hundred mark the jungle was a vast forcing house. Inevitably there was death and decay among all this life and the air was heavy with the sweet, damp smell of rotting vegetation. It was not unlike the strong smell of cabbages; but there was more to it, peppery and musty ingredients. It seemed to fill one's nostrils and lungs and to get right into one's stomach.

The jungle houses pests and parasites by the million, and from many of these we suffered badly. We were perpetually plagued by aggressive red ants whose bites were quite painful. There were leeches always alert to fasten themselves to our sweating bodies. These were the cause of jungle sores which eventually became skin ulcers which never healed up.

Ordinary flies seemed to swarm in the jungle. They settled on everything and were responsible very largely for the spread of dysentery. But by far the most dangerous were the mosquitoes. They carried both benign and malignant (cerebral) malaria. This was the greatest scourge of all. Eventually we all succumbed because it was impossible to take anything like adequate protective measures. The Japs issued a small number of Japanese quinine pills. Our own medical officers inspected these and said they were rubbish. Perhaps that was why they were passed on to us.

Not that we were the only sufferers, though most of the time it was easy to form this impression because we saw so little of the other jungle slaves. Occasionally, however, we did, and it was a salutary lesson.

One evening when we were dragging ourselves back to our camp, sullen with sheer weariness and self-pity, we came upon a party of

British other ranks. They were sitting or were stretched out on the side of the track just outside the Tonchan area and were apparently on their way up-country. Even the near darkness couldn't hide their pathetic, emaciated condition. They were in rags and nearly all of them obviously down with some sickness or other.

It seemed that the officer had gone off to get orders from the Japs, leaving the sergeant-major in charge. He was standing in the road, a tattered and bedraggled bulldog but still with some fight in him.

In a hoarse voice he was shouting at his charges, "'Ardships? 'ardships, you bastards! You don't know what bleedin' 'ardships are!"

To me it seemed a tough and harsh way of getting people to snap out of self-pity, but he seemed to be having some success, so perhaps he wasn't too far adrift in his rough wisdom. I suspect that he was finding it difficult to sustain his fighting manner.

His words and appearance made a strong impression on us. We held our aching bodies a little straighter, tried to turn our slouches into strides. We'd realized that we were not the only sufferers.

Some of the rumours we heard about the Burma campaign were reasonably accurate. The Imperial Japanese Army was in difficulties with its supplies. The Allied submarines were taking a heavy toll of shipping and acute shortages were developing. On paper, and disregarding the expert opinion of various engineers, the railway from Siam was the answer. The original Siam state railway ended at Bampong. The Japanese plan had been to extend this via Kanburi to Three Pagodas Pass on the Siam–Burma frontier. It meant working roughly northwards and parallel with the lowest strip of Burma – Tenasserim – from which there was the formidable barrier of the Bilauktaung Range.

The labour was at hand, in the shape of prisoners-of-war and Tamil coolies who could be forced to work for the New Order in Asia. Although all this was logical enough in theory, in practice it became as blundering and lunatic as the routine counting of prisoners.

The Jap high command was feverishly impatient to have the new railway in working order so that the essential fodder for their war machine could reach Burma. Yet they tried to achieve this with an undernourished force of men who were only fit for a convalescent home. Among ourselves it was often debated that the Japs didn't want the railway, but were using it as a means of exterminating their equally unwanted prisoners without any wastage of ammunition. It certainly looked that way; but there was a fanatical driving force which somehow spread right down to the most uncouth Korean guard. All our captors were in a hurry, though it was usually a directionless and senseless rush. Hardly a day passed without some ugly incident, some bestial outrage on a prisoner.

Of all the back-breaking hard labour we had to endure on the railway the worst in my opinion was the carrying of heavy teak tree trunks from the point where they had been felled down a steep, slippery path for about three-quarters of a mile to the Tonchan Saw Mill.

We were paraded at dawn and marched uphill on a path to the felling area. The work party consisted of fifty officers, twenty-five allotted to each side of the trunk. There was one large, heavy crowbar issued to each pair of officers. It was usually on the word of command "one, two three, *lift*!" after the crowbar had been pushed evenly under the trunk, that the nightmare began in earnest. Off we would go, staggering, sliding and slipping down the path.

It was extremely dangerous. Many lost their foothold and grip and a rogue trunk would go careering off down the bank on its own, travelling quite a distance, until it eventually crashed into one side of the jungle. At this point the guards would lose their tempers and indulge in an orgy of face-slapping and beating with bamboo sticks. When the uproar had subsided we would go through the whole wretched procedure again. "One, two, three, *lift*!"

We all agreed that this was a very hazardous occurrence and everyone thought that the best thing to do was to jump clear sideways. I think this must have given the guards the idea that we did it on purpose, hence the vicious attacks. We had to make as many journeys as possible in daylight, and as the day wore on until evening our journeys became fewer and fewer, resulting in the usual cries of "*Speedo, Speedo, Buggeroh!*" from the implacable guards.

Only those too ill to be able to stand were excused this trunk-moving labour and it went on every day with never a break. Our numbers were naturally depleted by sickness, and as the rest of us became weaker it became necessary for more and more to be assigned to the lifting of each trunk. In the end even this failed.

It was at this point that the Japs brought on the elephants, each under the direction of a Thai mahout.

Their arrival made a tremendous difference to our labours, for all we had to do was to attach the spikes and chains from the elephant's harness to the tree trunk. The mahout working with my particular party was a wizened little Thai. He looked for all the world like a monkey when he was crouched on the elephant's back. He guided the animal by pulling on either the right or left ear, and he always started up by prodding the poor beast with a spiked bar. It looked cruel but I was assured by those with experience of elephants that the prod was no more than a pinprick.

As the elephant lumbered off we followed up, occasionally using our weight to swing the tree a little in order to keep it on a straight course. The hardest moment for us was when we were at the saw and had to lift the tree-trunk to the saw bench. But this was nothing compared with the back-breaking work from which the elephant had now spared us. We were always patting Jumbo (who was, I believe, a female actually) and I think she knew, in some uncanny way, that we were trying to express gratitude. We could have forgiven her anything. Sometimes, as we followed right behind her, she would break wind loudly, almost in our faces; but this we treated as a joke.

As a result of this particular form of torture I developed a double hernia. The M.O. said it was not life-threatening and that many people in ordinary circumstances managed to live with it. Anyway, he said I would have to wait until the end of the war for repair surgery (God only knew when that would be). Nevertheless, I could manage if I was careful, although I was always conscious of it. In retrospect I think I must have grown to forget about it, as more horrible disorders began to take precedence.

There was no doubt that, owing to lack of supplies and planning, the railway was not proceeding as the Japs would have wished. It is interesting to note that, as the workforce diminished through sickness or death, the Japanese finally decided to use elephants for tree trunk labour. Had they done so earlier on, they might have saved a lot of lives, but it became more and more obvious they were not in the business of saving lives. If the Japanese had been more humane they might have operated their slave labour camps more efficiently. As it was, the whole railway was so badly built that it could never be operated properly.

This was borne out by the fact that one night a locomotive was derailed just north of our camp at Tonchan. It was well past midnight and most of us were exhausted and trying to get some sleep if possible. We were chased out of our miserable hovels and old tent coverings and herded down to the rail tracks. After strenuous efforts with chains and large iron levers we managed to get the engine back on the rails. I thought in retrospect that this was similar to the ancient Egyptian method of deploying slave labour: sheer weight of manpower as opposed to any mechanical aid such as lifting gear.

We reached a spiritual and physical rock-bottom while we were engaged on manhandling the heavy teak trunks to the saw-mill. Some days our work was a bit lighter, for instead of logs we carried the sleepers which had been sawn from them. These had to be taken and placed out along the cutting or embankment where the coolie gangs laboured. These were Tamils from the camp near to our own.

Their work was perhaps even harder than ours, for they were mostly digging a cutting through undulating ground. Tamils normally look thin and long-limbed. Under their present conditions they were gangling skeletons. They suffered appalling privations and ill-treatment. This we learnt because one or two of our Indian Army officers were former planters and could speak Tamil.

There was no shadow of doubt that all of them would have given anything to return to the much-maligned British Raj. They hated the Japs and everything to do with the New Order in Asia.

Yet these were some of the very people from whom the Japs expected loyalty and enthusiastic co-operation. To the Western mind it was all very incomprehensible, though, in fairness to the Japs, it must be recalled that the Axis allies were committing similar blunders.

We were particularly sorry for these Tamils, for their apathy and loss of will to live were pathetically obvious. They were, in fact, the first in Tonchan to contract cholera and they went down like flies.

But to return to our own troubles. In the midst of all the gruelling work our rice ration was cut to eight ounces a day and the only extra was that a few green leaves were thrown in. We cooked them with the rice, but they didn't seem to make much difference.

"They'll expect us to eat flaming grass next," one of the Australians remarked sourly.

We'd tried, so far as we dared, to make official complaints about the food cuts, but it wasn't worth the trouble. The inevitable answer was that things would be better when the trains could reach us, bringing better rations and more supplies. This would happen 'asta' – tomorrow.

By the time we reached this jungle camp we had all been in captivity some fifteen months, suffered hardships on one labouring task or another, and all had long spells on meagre and unsuitable rations. In consequence, before we started this dawn-to-dusk hard labour there wasn't a man among us who could be regarded as reasonably fit. The exhaustion of the long night marches and the effects of living in the open for the first days in Tonchan had resulted in widespread sickness of one sort or another. Looking back, I'm amazed that we did manage to carry on. Perhaps it was our one luxury, a mug of black tea, which did the trick. In justice to the Japs, supplies were short. It was not that they were being withheld by our taskmasters; it was simply that very little stuff was reaching Tonchan.

There was another party belonging to H Force following behind us. They were laying the rails and started at Tarsao about the time we started cutting the sleepers and levelling the track. There seemed an absence of overall command, in spite of the fact that the railway was a number one military priority. This resulted in shortages and also in a lot of labour being wasted or duplicated.

One day we were, to our astonishment, dismissed early and told we could go back to our camp. This was only a ruse. We didn't stop at our camp but continued past it on the way to Tarsao where a lorry loaded with sacks of rice had got stuck in the mud. We tried to move the lorry but couldn't free it so the only alternative was to carry the sacks on our backs.

They were heavy. Only the day before I'd started my first bout of malaria and I felt terribly weak. Bent under the weight I could virtually feel that I was crumbling up. Each step was unsteadier than the last and I couldn't avoid reeling from one side of the track to the other. At last I fell. I struggled to get to my feet, but couldn't manage it.

As I lay there I could see the rays of the sun as it was setting on the higher hills across the valley. It was a beautiful sight, with all the rich colouring of tropical sunset contrasting with the sombre grandeur of the greenish blacks of impenetrable jungle.

I knew that I couldn't get up. The thought crossed my mind that I was probably going to die. It didn't seem as important as the sunset, or the sunsets of which it reminded me, those of my boyhood when I had looked across Dartmoor. How refreshing it would be if only that chill Dartmoor mist could sweep across me and banish my fever.

Perhaps I was very near to death because I seemed to float between past and present as if the real me was trying to escape from the fatigue-tormented hulk which fettered it. Tears streamed down my face as the Jap sentry came up to me, his face contorted with rage. After barking incomprehensible orders he kicked me, then beat me with a bamboo cane until I was semi-consciousness. I honestly thought he was going to kill me, but eventually he left after giving me a few farewell kicks in the groin. This resulted in permanent injury, which I have to this day, to my scrotum and testicles.

For some time after I suffered excruciating pains in my groin and also a stabbing pain in my side. It was only after the war, when we were given chest X-Rays by the Red Cross, that I discovered I had suffered a fractured rib which had self-healed, albeit in a misshapen manner causing a deformity.

I lay prostrate on the corner of the track and there suddenly appeared round it a bedraggled little group in shabby bush hats. I had another moment of clarity and recognized them. There was good old Bert Savile and with him John Norbury, Spike Grieve and Peter Playfair.

They trudged up to me and stopped. One of them, I'm not sure which, turned to the Nip sentry and said menacingly, "Bugger off!"

Perhaps the quartet looked dangerously villainous even to an armed sentry. He departed.

The four turned their attention to me. 'Come on, Reg, you'll be okay with us."

They lifted my rice sack, quickly and efficiently redistributed their loads, and then gently lifted me. So with my burden of rice I was carried back to Tonchan. Here I was put to bed, laid low by the ravages of malaria and my injuries.

I believe I had been very near death, if not from injury and disease then from the Jap, who might well have shot me for failing to obey an order. I'd also, in those brief sunset moments, had a vision of beauty which transcended the filth and ugliness of my circumstances. And then that filth and ugliness was defeated by the compassion and help of the four tough Australians, or four good Samaritans would be the best description. Perhaps, as there was still such goodness in the world, there was also some hope of survival.

# Chapter 7

## EVACUATION FROM HELL

## DECEMBER 1943

There was to be none of the rest which my body craved. I had one day of only partial consciousness which was spent in bed. The panic to get ahead with the railway was working like a fever on the Japs and they decreed that all men must turn out and labour. So I was returned to duty.

In this I was not singularly unfortunate. There were many other sufferers in just as bad a condition, and the majority of us would have been classified as hospital bed cases by British Army medical standards.

Sometimes the worst of the sick were left in camp. This was entirely dependant on the capricious decision of the Korean private detailed to round up the working parties. If he was smarting from the hard words or blows of his Japanese engineer bosses he'd take it out on those of us who were sick, going through the tents and huts kicking everyone out on to the parade ground. The Senior British Officer, the medical officer, and an interpreter would do their best for the men who were obviously unfit, but any intervention inevitably finished up in a face-slapping orgy.

I don't know how I managed to parade. Those near me helped me to keep on my feet. But the greatest help was to come from Major 'Uncle' Evans, our Gurkha commanding officer. Uncle Evans fought a truly magnificent battle against the Japs and knew every trick it was possible to pull. With some of the parties that went out there were a few much-prized jobs which called for no great amount of physical exertion. On this occasion he had contrived to enter my name on the nominal roll as an Engineer. This meant that I could sit, with a blanket around me, and keep up a pretence of watching the wretched contraption miscalled a generator. This supplied electricity to the arc lamps over the cutting, where some of our own chaps from H 6 had now been ordered to join the Tamils in all-night work.

This new decree was part of the general feverishness to make some real progress with the railway. What had been done so far couldn't have looked very impressive on the map. It was highly probable that someone at H.Q. of the Imperial Japanese Army had lost his temper and kicked someone. The kicking had continued downwards and had now reached us, the labourers, the lowest form of life.

The cutting on which work was now directed was being hacked out of solid rock so that the railway could eventually traverse the shoulder of a mountain. The treatment meted out by the Korean guards was more bestial than ever. If a man, white or Tamil, was caught slacking, even through illness, he was forced to stand holding a rock high above his head. This was a fiendishly cruel punishment because it was extended over long periods, and when the exhausted victim dropped his arms he was beaten with crowbars.

There was, on this sector, one especially inhuman guard who used to move around the labouring gangs lashing out at them with a golf club.

It was a gloomy thought that my easier job meant light was being provided for such slavery and cruelty. I wished the whole contraption would blow up, provided the other sick officer helping me and I were out of range.

The generator consisted of an internal combustion engine which was tended by my fellow sufferer, and this drove a dynamo which had a series of dials giving the output in volts and amps. There were other dials, but in spite of the claim made on the nominal roll I didn't understand them in the slightest.

One night there was an appalling commotion. The lights failed. The petrol engine was chugging contentedly away and driving the dynamo.

I fiddled around a bit, but to my consternation none of my experimental efforts produced a renewal of light. My blanketed companion was no wiser than I. There were a few others in our party in the vicinity but there wasn't an expert among them.

A Jap sentry arrived in a tearing hurry and I expected to be shot. He barked a whole range of invective against me. About the only bit I understood was the frequently repeated "Ingrisu shoko Bugero-kurrah", which was an impolite way of saying that "English officer bloody fool". At last a Japanese engineer officer arrived. There must have been a number of these officers, but they were a rare sight on the actual workings. This one was grinning – a certain indication of anger and displeasure. However, he ignored me after this and indulged in what seemed a heated argument with the Jap sentry. This became so tremendous an affair that I quite expected to see the Jap sentry shot. However, the fuss died down and the necessary repair was effected by the Jap sentry under instructions from the engineer officer.

It was good to have the tension relieved, but I anticipated some severe punishment, if only for disturbing a Japanese engineer officer.

My companion was equally apprehensive, though I think he was too ill, poor fellow, to know much of what was going on. Like myself he was a malaria case, but his attack was really severe. He stayed huddled in his blanket shaking with the rigors. He was an officer from the Indian Army and he died shortly after this incident.

The sentry returned with a blow-lamp which he lit and pumped to maximum heat. He hadn't looked at me and I began to get some shivers which had nothing to do with my malaria. This looked uncommonly like a prelude to some Oriental torture, like burning the soles of the feet.

But to my amazement he took a steel helmet, poured the contents of a tin of condensed milk into it, and heated it over the blow-lamp. When it was hot he offered it to me and the other sick officer. We accepted with gratitude, but without understanding. Perhaps it was an apology for having been rude. Perhaps it was an indirect admission that no guilt could be attached to us for the temporary breakdown.

So far as my experience ran Japs did have this extraordinary characteristic of indulging in some simple act of kindness, such as offering a cigarette or a banana, after a display of violent temper or frightful act of brutality. The cruelty seemed spontaneous rather than organized. I once saw a Jap corporal turn on a Jap private and beat him senseless with a bamboo pole. After this he marched away and left the other privates to carry off their unconscious companion.

In general, so far as I saw it, their treatment of their fellow Asians was more overbearing and brutal than their attitude to us. This was particularly true in the cruelty they showed to the civilian coolies who were officially a labour force to the Imperial Japanese Army Siam Command.

We of H Force, incidentally, were on loan from Malaya Command to Siam Command and this, for a time, resulted in getting the worst of both worlds. Malay Command had virtually washed their hands of us. Siam Command didn't care what happened to us because they were not going to retain our services after the railway construction was completed. The same applied to F Force.

We benefited from this arrangement ultimately, for when the railway was completed those of us who survived were returned to Singapore and civilization. Other PoW parties who set up the base camps and were actually under Siam Command fared a bit better, because they manned these bases and received certain 'perks', but they were doomed to spend their entire war in Siam's jungles.

My malaria eased off after several days and nights of alternating between feverishness and shivering. There was very little the M.O. could do for me. He had a small bottle of those Japanese quinine pills, which really had proved to be useless. However, they were doled out sparingly to those men with rigors in the hope they'd give a little ease to the suffering.

Of course, the ideal would have been to have taken steps to prevent malaria. Tablets given as a routine would have achieved a lot. However, there wasn't much the M.O. could do. He hadn't even a sufficient quantity of the worthless tablets. It seemed most unlikely that these had been manufactured especially for prisoners-of-war and when the Japs distributed the small quantity they decided they could spare for us I had the impression they believed they were being helpful. The obvious conclusion is that some Japanese industrialists were not above adding to their profits at the expense of their own army.

One of our humorists commented, "So solly – big mistake – forgot to put quinine in tablets."

Our own medical officers had a hopeless task. They were without bandages. In order to place coverings over our jungle sores and ulcers, which were increasing in number and size, they were reduced to the expedient of using green leaves and cutting strips from old tents and boiling the canvas in order to sterilize and soften it.

Back to full duty in the slave gang I lost all sense of the passage of the days. There was nothing to distinguish one from another. There was the same miserable food, the same rotting-vegetation smell of the jungle, the same shuffling march and the same weary work, day after day with never a break.

One day, when we'd penetrated deeper into the jungle, we came upon the droppings of some animal and one of the Indian Army officers who'd often been on shikar in peacetime immediately identified it as evidence of tiger. It gave us an uneasy feeling, because we'd sufficient jungle experience by this time to know how expert wild creatures were at concealing themselves. Although we heard so many of them at night, we saw surprisingly few during the day. We often had a rather uncanny feeling that we were being watched and I expect this was frequently true. Fortunately we never encountered a tiger. We warned the Korean sentry and he was sufficiently alarmed to tell the others, because next time out they all carried rifles.

The Australians insisted we had nothing to fear. No tiger was going to feed on living skeletons when there were a few fat bastards of Koreans around. Not that our guards looked particularly well fed in fact. They were more or less pariah dogs living on scraps from the Japanese table.

One evening we managed something much better than scraps. The railway line had still not reached Tonchan South and it was no unusual sight for us to see long columns of Jap troops, with their supplies in trains of bullock carts, making a gruelling march into Burma. We used to watch the troops with a sort of cold hatred and I'm sure each one of us wished them ill in the fighting ahead. Had we known how many were to perish we would have felt a grim satisfaction.

On this particular occasion there were a few stragglers in the bullock train. The exhausted animals were being unmercifully beaten with sticks wielded by their Jap drivers.

It is perhaps worth mentioning that the Japs took a stick to anything that wouldn't go, whether it was a white PoW or a Tamil, or an animal. We once came upon a Jap soldier stolidly beating the radiator of a lorry which had broken down. John Norbury, one of our irrepressible Australians, nearly caused us to die with the effort of stifling laughter. He stepped across to the Jap and in a most serious manner drawled, "I reckon I can help you, Nippon."

'Ah – so – ka?" The Jap was interested.

'What sort of stick are you using?"

The Jap understood and produced an ordinary short piece of stick which John Norbury solemnly examined, shaking his head slowly. "This is no use, Nippon. You have to use bamboo. Much better."

The Jap provided himself with one and proceeded to chastise the radiator. We moved on as swiftly as we could, still convulsed with laughter.

We didn't feel like laughing, though, as we witnessed the cruel treatment the poor bullocks were suffering. The last cart in the line was some distance behind the others and the wretched animal trying to draw it was just tottering, right out on its feet. Painfully it drew level with our cookhouse, where Old Bert and Spike were standing. They joined the others in abuse of the cursing and furiously angry Jap who was still walloping the obviously dying animal.

"Leave the poor bloody beast to die, Nippon!"

"Turn it up! She's gone crook on you."

"Can't you see she's finished, you stupid bastard?"

And indeed it was the end for the animal. It stumbled and died in its traces within a yard or so of Old Bert and Spike. There were no other Japs in sight. The ape-like waggoner looked around him, his brutish little mind obviously trying to work out what to do. Instead of going back to the guardroom of our camp for help, he decided to run after the column and ask for fresh orders – no doubt after getting his face slapped for turning up minus bullock and cart. This meant that he was away for quite twenty minutes.

The Australians, under the leadership of Old Bert, went into action. I watched, amazed. I couldn't have helped; I'd only have been in the way. The dead bullock was whipped out of its harness and into the surrounding bushes. The carcass was cut up, the horns, hoofs, bones and skin were buried. We had some large *quailis* – these were large iron bowls for cooking our rice and were shaped like an enormous British steel helmet turned upside down. The meat was covered with a film of rice. Fortunately the fires had only just been lit, so it was safe to place the big cooking bowls on them without there being any betraying meaty odours.

All this was finished and we were back in our original positions, doing our camp chores by the time the Jap driver returned. With him there was a corporal and an escort of Jap soldiers. They came to the cart and halted.

We all pretended that we had no interest, but every man was watching out of the corners of his eyes. Suddenly there was bedlam, all the Japs shouting at once. We couldn't follow the arguments, but everybody seemed to be blaming everybody else. Evidently the upshot of this angry debate was that they believed the animal had risen to its feet, unharnessed itself and strolled off into the darkness.

102

They spread out and started to search, positively beating the bushes.

It was an irresistible opportunity for a display of British and Australian stupidity.

"Lost something, Nippon?" somebody called, starting the game.

The result was plenty of abuse and then some quick-fire questions. We scratched our heads. We went into mock-serious discussion. Then we tried to convey that we didn't understand what the Japs were talking about. We hadn't seen a bullock wandering around. Had there been one pulling the cart? There had!

"Beats me!"

The Japs fanned out and searched everywhere, and we had a few bad moments when they were near our cooking pots. But they were looking for a whole bullock, not one that had been cut up, so not one of them was inquisitive about what might be in the pots.

At last the Jap corporal evidently felt uneasy at having dropped so far behind the column. He barked some orders and the ex-waggoner and the privates stepped into the traces and started to haul the cart along.

They were given tremendous vocal encouragement from "Yo ho, heave ho!" to a spirited rendering of "Volga Boatmen". We had all enjoyed ourselves thoroughly at the expense of the Japs, especially as our bullock was beginning to smell appetising. And that night was memorable for its supper of wholesome beef stew.

But not all our evenings were so amusing. There was one in which a discussion concerning our miserable lot was followed by tragedy. We'd consumed our meagre meal and our stomachs still felt empty. Someone asked if the rest of us thought this could go on for ever. Perhaps we were prisoners in an unending war. If so, another answered, we might as well be dead. If there was nothing but this ahead of us, the quicker we were out of it the better. Why go on suffering and being half-starved?

We finished on a note of optimism. Our lot would probably improve when the trains reached us and there were more regular lines of communication.

We'd talked ourselves sleepy and one by one we dropped off – with one exception.

I was awakened by a gurgling noise which was pretty horrible. There was a scuffling just outside the tent. This awakened us all. Two, nearer the door, went outside. They were quickly back.

"For God's sake don't go out there," one said.

The other explained. One of the young officers who'd joined in that discussion had tried to commit suicide by cutting his throat with a razor. He was being rushed across to the M.O.

Had the rest of us contributed? Had our discussion been unwise? I think we all felt a little guilty.

Our emotions differed again a few nights later. We were to witness a distressing sight, though even in this there was to be a moment of humour. Huddled in my blanket, I was watching the dials on the wretched generator when the order came to stop work. We were cautioned to keep silent. We grouped together, wondering what this meant.

Then, out of the darkness, there came a long column of our fellow prisoners-of-war, British and Australian. They were newcomers, suffering the same distress from night marching that we had suffered. It was impossible to obey the order to remain silent. The Jap guards, infuriated, beat us on the back with bamboos, but they failed to quieten us.

We called out greetings and encouragement. Some of us, recognizing a prisoner, would ask after other friends. I watched the pitiful straggling column closely, but I saw no Royal Norfolks or Suffolks. There seemed to be men, though, from every other unit or regiment that had been stationed in Malaya. Their uniforms were ragged and their hats would have made a fantastic collection, for they ranged from old trilbys to home-made jockey caps.

Among the prisoners was one immense Australian, a real giant. He ambled along clad only in a slouch hat, Jantzen swimming trunks and boots. He carried a small pack, a rice bowl and a staff. There was loud applause for him. He was known to some of our Australians and I gathered that he was by trade a blacksmith from the outback.

Among the greetings someone shouted, "Hey, Joe! Where d'ya think you're heading – Juan-les-Pins?"

He acknowledged everything with a boxer's handclasp. I admired his great-hearted cheerfulness.

The long column went past. Our shouts died down. Beaten and prodded with bamboos, we returned to work, our hatred towards our captors burning more strongly than ever.

Watching these white slaves moving up-country to body- and spirit-killing labour was a harrowing experience, however much we tried to hide our feelings and give them what encouragement we could. But there was something infinitely more harrowing to come.

We paraded one morning and were starting our march to work when, in the gathering light, we had a glimpse of the Tamil compound. To our horror we saw that it was littered with bodies. Uncle Evans halted us while he went off to complain to the Japs. The Tamils were obviously dead and it was not a climate in which bodies should be left for long unburied. The Jap reply was that if we wanted to make a fuss about it, the best thing we could do was to go and bury them. We were excused from other work.

This was the most horrible and macabre task that ever came my way. When we approached the Tamil camp we stood for a few moments rooted to the ground, holding our breath, fighting down an urge to vomit. Over the jungle smell of rotting vegetation hung the ghastly stench of death. There were black bodies lying everywhere, emaciated bodies with their skeleton-like limbs spread grotesquely. It was worse than anything Dante pictured. This was a real glimpse into hell after the torture of the damned.

Even those of us with little medical knowledge knew what had killed the Tamils. It confirmed ugly rumours which had reached us recently. This was cholera!

The natural impulse was to turn and run from the spot. Our medical officers quickly realized this reaction and assured us that cholera was essentially a water-borne infection, entering the body through the nose or the mouth. Touching the germs by hand would not in itself convey infection. But we must be careful, once we'd started our grim task, not to put our hands to our mouths.

Someone said, wisely, "The longer we hold back the worse this is going to get."

We drew spades, pickaxes and stretchers. Then we moved into the Tamil camp among the dead. We were told to fold a handkerchief or other strip of material over our faces, but scarcely anybody had such a possession. So the Japs brought along a stirrup pump and sprayed us with a Japanese disinfectant. I took my spraying and hoped the stuff was more effective than their malaria tablets.

The entire morning was spent in digging a large, square pit. With the heat of the day the stench increased, for the bodies were lying in pools of liquid vomit and excretion. The flies were attracted and swarmed in their thousands.

By afternoon the pit was completed. We were paired off with stretchers and my companion was an Irish-American Merchant Navy officer named Kellaher, who was nick-named Kelly. He was a truly tough character and some of his comments helped to keep me going.

There was an appalling feeling of being naked and unprotected as we picked our way among the corpses. Some were not quite corpses, they were still twitching in death agony. Others moved a little in death as *rigor mortis* set in.

Over the first one that we lifted to the stretcher I nearly gave in and vomited. Kelly steadied me. I held my breath and as my fingers touched the naked black flesh of the dead Tamil I had the feeling that some form of leprosy was creeping up my arms. This had to have been the lowest depth so far and I felt that my very sanity was threatened. I wanted to run screaming from the ghastly clearing.

But I didn't. I helped Kelly with the stretcher and we set off with our burden towards the pit, where we tipped it in. Then we turned and went to collect another. Gradually the ground was cleared of the dead. I felt pity for these cholera victims, but at the same time I hated them. I wanted them destroyed, burnt up, anything to get them out of sight. Their uncleanliness had spread to me and I felt I should never rid myself of it.

Kelly maintained his grim humour. One of our burdens started to twitch and he said, "Oh boy. Dis stiff is still movin' – let's take him back." But there was nowhere we could take him. Assuming there was still a flicker of life, it was on its way out. So we dumped this body into the pit with the others.

At last the dreadful task was ended. The bodies in the pit were covered with quicklime and the earth was hastily thrown on top. There was no service. I felt there should have been a prayer, even though a Christian prayer wouldn't mean much to a Hindu soul. However, I said one to myself. My revulsion was dying down now that the bodies were out of sight and I could feel pity for those who had laboured with us on the hellish railway.

Their deaths, it must be said, had come about largely because of ignorance and lack of hygiene. It was obviously necessary for us to take every precaution to keep the dread disease at bay. We washed in disinfectant and the little white-coated Jap, his face mostly hidden by a gauze mask, sprayed us again. Then we were permitted to return to our camp.

We'd had nothing to eat all day, so there was extra rice. We'd finished earlier than usual and I suppose this brief extra rest was our reward for doing the Japs' unsavoury work for them. At first, with the stench of death still in my nostrils, I felt I wouldn't be able to touch food, but after an exploratory mouthful I fed as heartily as everybody else.

Our Medical Officers were certain that the cholera had been brought down the valley by the stream. They considered the river also was contaminated. This resulted in placing both out of bounds. We were put on a ration of one water-bottle full of boiled water per day for each of us. There was absolute insistence that no other water should come in contact with vital orifices. This meant that shaving, washing the face, and cleaning the teeth were strictly forbidden, unless one was prepared to sacrifice some of the boiled water.

These stringent precautions undoubtedly saved our lives. While I was there not a single officer went down with cholera. Understanding the risks, we obeyed the orders strictly and there was no need for the type of supervision which might in normal circumstances have been necessary. So, along with the others, I reserved the precious supply of safe water for drinking. I grew a black beard and I must have looked particularly villainous because my teeth went black.

As a result of the cholera risk our losing battle against personal vermin such as lice became an outright defeat. These caused skin rashes which never healed properly and became septic. Another skin trouble, caused by dirt and minute parasites, was scabies. We did our best to keep these in check by washing as often as possible and boiling our clothes in a bucket. But the water situation brought an end to all this. We were not able to rid ourselves of vermin until our return to civilization. I often sighed for my primitive de-lousing machine.

About this time I calculated that it was somewhere near my birthday – we were rarely sure of the exact date. I was feeling rather low in spirits. Our rations had been low. These tended to fluctuate. Sometimes we had just the bare eight ounces of rice, then suddenly this would be increased to ten with a few greens thrown in. It was also possible, at certain times, to obtain boiled eggs. Even here there was a black market which operated sporadically. So to celebrate my birthday I at last parted with my gold wrist watch. This my mother had given me for Christmas in 1933, which now seemed another existence ago, and I'd treasured it highly. I'd always been careful to keep it out of sight from the prying eyes of thieving Jap soldiers, for it was not unknown for them to force prisoners to part with such possessions by threats and intimidation. But now, when there seemed no future, when any day might be the last, hunger prevailed over sentiment. I passed on the watch to an Indian Army officer who had a contact. With the twenty Ticals proceeds – no questions asked – we were able to buy some hard-boiled eggs and John and I celebrated my birthday.

This was the last celebration at Tonchan South for me. There was a swift deterioration in my health. The bouts of violent shivering increased. The M.O. swiftly diagnosed blackwater fever. There were other things wrong with me and I had a bad bout of beri-beri. My face and my ankles were swollen, the latter so badly that I was unable to walk. I tried several times to get to the latrines but always fell over. I was moved to a better tent and put near the door because I was gasping for breath.

While I was in this sorry condition the Japanese at last agreed to start evacuating the bad cases of sickness as soon as the railway reached us. On that day the rice was improved by bits of fried liver. It was the first enjoyable meal since the bullock had provided a stew. But I couldn't eat it.

I was having bouts of delirium, not knowing where I was or who those about me were. I can recall one vivid nightmare. I was trying to sleep in a dried river bed where all the rocks were sharp and jagged. Japs were beating me with red hot pokers, but I couldn't move.

My evacuation to the train is something of which I have only a vague memory. John and a few of my other friends came to see me off. Among others who were being taken back to civilization was a Corporal Watson. He was a military policeman whose home was in Bradford. Throughout the long journey he looked after me like a guardian angel, perhaps a surprising role for a military policeman.

These were the lost days. After getting aboard the train I knew virtually nothing of what was happening. There were a few isolated moments of vague consciousness, leaving no clear impression. I was told afterwards that I'd suffered delirium, sinking at intervals into a coma. I suppose I'd reached the limit of exhaustion. In this way I left the jungle, and the hellish toil in unspeakably foul conditions. But I didn't know what was going on, or that I was involved in it. I do have one dim memory of being on firm ground again, of being supported as I struggled along a track. This led from a railway siding to a hutted camp, but I was in no state to realize anything beyond the fact that I was being forced to move and that it was an ordeal. I escaped from it into blackness and it was much like drifting away from a disturbing dream.

My first real memory is a strange one. There was dim lighting from a coconut oil lamp. I lay for a little time becoming aware of this. I was inside an atap hut. With my mind clearing I regained a little strength and was able to move my body and sit up. To my astonishment I saw a young Tamil woman on the other side of the hut. She was naked and was combing her long black tresses.

I can recall the effort of trying to work out what all this meant. Who I was – whether I was still me. This could be after death and, if so, I'd wandered into the ante-chamber of some other religion.

It was like trying to fit an alien piece into a jigsaw puzzle. The shape and the colours were wrong. My memory, however, began to work sluggishly and I did realize that I was on my way out of a truly terrible situation where death would very soon have been my lot.

There was no more. I suppose I dropped back and lost consciousness. I've no idea how long that interval of awareness lasted but I suppose, as the not unattractive Tamil girl had given no sign of even knowing I was in the hut, that it was of very short duration.

I was taken back to the train again, because my next moment of clarity was when I was being lifted from the railway truck and set down on a grassy bank. It was night. For the first time since my fevered deliriums had started I felt cool. I lay looking up at the stars and thinking how miraculously peaceful everything was. I was still wet with sweat but I was no longer burning. I felt I could stay here for ever.

This was probably the turning point in my condition. We had, during my period of lost consciousness, come from Tonchan to a Tamil coolie camp in Tarsao. That journey had taken two days and a night, I learnt later. We were now at Tamarkand Bridge Camp.

There were many others lying around on the same grassy bank this night. Gradually they were moved as stretcher parties came up with them. Eventually it was my turn. Corporal Watson, who'd looked after me painstakingly during the worst hours, was near. He satisfied himself that I was comfortably on a stretcher before he went off.

The journey on the stretcher was only a short one. We came to a camp and I was taken into a long, low atap hut and placed near the end. There were a few lights and in this semi-darkness I could see a small group who seemed to be in charge of everything that was going on. Their obvious chief was a sunburnt, fair-haired man clad only in white shorts. When he came nearer I could see that he was quite good-looking.

He introduced himself as Lt.-Col. Philip Toosey, the C.O. of this camp, Tamarkand Bridge, which was a fairly well organized hospital camp. Like all the other hospitals for prisoners-of-war it was fantastically short of necessary medical equipment and supplies. So to achieve any degree of organization called for superhuman ingenuity and improvisation.

The C.O. spoke kindly to me, assured me that I was out of danger and would soon be on my feet again. It was probably a formality, for the doctor had yet to examine me, but it was tremendously encouraging. I'd no power any longer to do anything on my own. I had to have others caring for me.

The C.O. was followed by an adjutant who, in the best military tradition, unruffled by the strangeness of these surroundings, wanted my particulars.

Finally the doctor looked at me. By this time I was very tired and my mind was playing tricks again. It was a fact that there was a resemblance between this doctor and my father, but in my half-delirium, and with the half-light inside the hut, I confused the two and I had the fantastic idea that somehow I'd been flown home.

My return to better health was painfully slow. I must add that I received the best treatment that was available. One incident shed light on the situation. I awakened one night and as the doctor was turning from me to speak to an orderly I heard him say, "This chap has a good chance. Give him . . ." I heard no more because, in spite of my interest, my body insisted on more sleep.

Undoubtedly, though, this fragment which I'd overheard referred to the limited supply of atabrin tablets. These were precious and I did receive a few. I've a pretty definite idea that they had to adopt a very realistic policy, assessing which patients had a chance of pulling through. Drugs which were so scarce couldn't be wasted on those who were inevitably going to die. Many of the poor devils who were brought down to this hospital were virtual corpses. Quite a number died on arrival and, indeed, some were lying dead in the trucks as the trains pulled into Tamarkand Bridge.

For me, more fortunate, the worst was over, although I was still in a very sorry state. There was the blackwater fever from relapsing malaria and I eventually contracted jaundice, though I believe this helped me for the following reason! There was little medicine available and I think it was the yellow bile in the bloodstream which killed the malarial parasites and so eventually cured me of this. I had other troubles, because I was also suffering from beri-beri. Below my knees my legs were horribly swollen, a typical symptom. This disease, of course, was the result of the long rice diet and the consequent vitamin B deficiency. This vitamin was present in the whole rice grain but eliminated when the rice was milled. Another result of this complaint was the swelling of my face. I must have presented a really ugly picture, because in addition to the puffy face I still had my black beard and my teeth were black. Some of my pals assured me I looked like Henry VIII, though I doubt whether the comparison would have pleased that monarch.

The atap hut which was my hospital ward was filled with British, Australian and American sufferers. They lay in rows down each side. There must have been cases of nearly every tropical disease, usually with complications, and we were gradually sorted out and classified under our diseases.

I remained here for several weeks and the medical orderly who attended me most of the time was a Malay named Jaleh. It's impossible to speak too highly of him. He was a private in the R.A.M.C. and because of his uniform he'd been taken into custody as a British soldier.

The majority of his fellows were regarded by the Japs as Malay colonial soldiers. Their units were disbanded and the men were returned to their kampongs. Jaleh could have joined them by exchanging his uniform for a sarong, but he stayed in the R.A.M.C. Later, I did my best to obtain promotion for him, putting forward the strongest recommendation I could. To my disgust it was a wasted effort. Jaleh had not sacrificed his freedom with the idea of reward and it seemed to me very niggling to give him no recognition. I wished those responsible for turning him down could have had to spend a few days in the conditions where he worked.

As I had difficulty in breathing I was put near the door of the hut. Although there were so many fellow-sufferers near to me I felt very much alone at first, because none of them could talk or give any indication of being interested in living. I found sleep difficult and at night I would lie for hours looking out through the doorway at the black outline of the craggy mountains.

I got accustomed to lying in the dark and trying to pick out the outline of the distant Thai mountains through the doorway of the atap hut. It gave me new hope, to wait and watch the first rays of dawn as the golden sun gradually appeared above the craggy peaks. I knew then that I had made it to another day and I would eventually recover. It helped me to remember some lines of the *Rubaiyat of Omar Khayyàm*.

> Awake! For Morning in the Bowl of Night
> Has flung the Stone that puts the Stars to Flight:
>   And Lo! the Hunter of the East has caught
> The Sultan's Turret in a Noose of Light.

This was a great noose of hope for me, as it turned out. Daytime became very strongly associated with living because it was during the night that the harvest of death seemed to be reaped. There was something of purgatory in the nightly scene. Men would cry out for help, or groan with pain. Doctors and orderlies would move quietly, and all too frequently the orderlies would depart carrying yet another lifeless figure. I often wondered how many of the poor wretches who died were, like me, waiting and hoping for the dawn.

Corporal Watson, who'd tended me during my complete helplessness on the journey south, had been moved to another ward on arrival. Jaleh took his place as my friend and comforter. At night he always found time to fill my water bottle with boiling water so that I could lie with its warmth soothing my stomach, but for much of the time there was nothing to relieve the loneliness and monotony. I used to watch for Jaleh's hurrying figure just so that I could wave to him. Sometimes he'd stop and talk to me. His lively chatter gave me new hope and strength.

He was there when I was at last allowed to struggle to my feet and try to walk a few steps. In spite of his attention, though, I fell over several times during my first efforts. Mentally, I was convinced I could walk, but my legs seemed to have different ideas altogether. Jaleh, who I'd repeatedly waved aside, would repeatedly have to help me up.

This first ward was really the arrival hut. All the new patients were brought here. Their complaints were diagnosed and they were given what preliminary treatment was possible, provided there was hope of survival. For the hopelessly doomed there was this last consolation of rest. For this reason, of course, the mortality rate was much higher than anywhere else in the hospital camp.

The day came when I was strong enough to go to the officers' ward on the other side of the camp. My stay in the arrival hut was rather

112

protracted because I was, I think, the only officer there and they'd decided to keep me until I could be sent to join my old friends. It saved an intermediate stage.

In my new quarters, to my great delight, I met John again. While not so seriously ill as I, his health had been poor and this, together with his gammy leg, eventually persuaded the Jap taskmasters that he was of very little use to them. So they'd sent him after me. Bert, the Australian old-timer, was here also. He'd been evacuated from Tonchan at the same time as John. Typically, he'd started running the officers' cookhouse and the older inhabitants of the ward declared the food had immediately started to improve.

There were many others from H 6 Force which, after I'd left it, had gone farther up the line and suffered more casualties. Their sufferings, though, seemed light by comparison with the ghastly stories which were coming through about F Force. It was said that, in checking the progress up the line, a Jap patrol group had come across a camp well up towards Three Pagodas Pass to find that approximately two hundred men had died of cholera. There were only two survivors and one of these had gone out of his mind.

There were other stories, equally grim.

From what I could remember, which was little, of my period of delirium I'd always been tortured by extreme heat. I was right up against a burning building, or actually on fire. I was being roasted in a large metal cattle truck. Arising from these I'd developed an unslakable thirst. I longed for fizzy lemonade and other sparkling minerals. The craving was so strong that at times it became an obsession. I suppose these were dehydration symptoms.

This craving was still with me when I met an old friend, Corporal Newsom (who back in the regiment had been nicknamed affectionately Corporal Nuisance). I'd just been moved to the officers' ward and he stepped into the hut. I was very pleased to see him and we swapped experiences. When I happened to mention the thirst craving he said he thought he could get me some lemonade. It seemed he had a job as a driver. I couldn't imagine that anything of this nature was obtainable in a place like Tamarkand Bridge Camp, but, true to his word, he came across one evening with two bottles of Siamese orangeade.

I was overjoyed. This was what I'd dreamed and almost raved about for weeks. However, I still don't know what Siamese orangeade tastes like because the medical officer caught me with a bottle and snatched it from my lips. He said the bottles might contain even worse bugs than the ones we had already.

As I regained some strength I was allowed to walk around the wards. I knew from experience what a difference a little company made. There wasn't very much that was useful that I could do. I discovered that "book readers" were in demand, so consequently I applied for and got the job. The book in question was a very grimy bethumbed paperback, Agatha Christie's *Murder on the Blue Train*. By the time I'd finished I think I almost knew it by heart.

In spite of my willingness to help I dreaded being detailed to the ulcer ward. I used to glue my eyes to the book and read on doggedly while the ulcers were being dressed. The sights were too ghastly for my stomach and the revolting stench was nearly as bad. In some cases leg ulcers had gone so far that it was actually possible to see daylight behind the shin bone.

So I droned on and on with the exploits of Hercule Poirot, interrupted now and then by the agonized groans of the patient. I often wondered how many really enjoyed the story.

It was possible to loathe the disease but to feel a compassionate affection towards the sufferers. In the ward there were rows and rows of pitiful human skeletons with their limbs almost eaten away by tropical sores and ulcers. The ravages were accelerated by malnutrition and neglect. The causes of these dreadful scourges were often no more than slight skin abrasions sustained when working in the jungle. The germs collected and multiplied in these immediately. I was punctured in my right upper forearm by a thorn while I was gathering wood in Tonchan South. Even this small scratch developed into an ulcer. Though it wouldn't heal up, it fortunately didn't get any worse. Most of the leg ulcers became so severe that skin and tissue were eaten away, revealing the bones of the leg. For some reason, certain people seemed to have a greater natural immunity to ulcers. Perhaps I was fortunate in this respect, though in others I was as wasted by tropical diseases as the next man.

It is not surprising that there were men who cracked up mentally. I doubt if any of us were completely sane. There were one or two who had to be kept under restraint and several who were moved to a special mental hut. It was from this, one day, that a bearded figure emerged. Clutching a staff, he called out that he was Jesus Christ and that he could walk away from captivity, even through the wire. He managed to evade those who tried to stop him and actually reached the wire. It was an ugly moment because the Jap sentries were watching him. They were on the point of shooting him down, in spite of our appeals, when our camp adjutant came running up and very bravely intervened.

All incidents didn't end so peacefully. One night we were all asleep in our ward when we were awakened by agonized screams coming from the direction of the Jap guardhouse. As these went on and on we turned out and tried to discover what was happening. There was a great deal of confusion but at last we obtained some reliable information.

Some of the patients who'd recovered sufficiently to be reasonably mobile had hatched up a plan for augmenting their meagre incomes. Although the Japs made some attempts to keep to the convention that prisoners-of-war should be paid, these were spasmodic and un- reliable. This made it very difficult to ration funds out, which meant that even when a few so-called luxuries were suddenly obtainable, there wasn't always the available cash.

The conspirators had, somehow, managed to contact the Thais outside the hospital and arranged a night meeting at the wire. They'd collected some Jap pickaxes, shovels and changgols – the latter a Malayan and Siamese spade-type implement used for hoeing. It was the intention to sell these over the wire, but the Jap sentries were on the alert and our men had been caught in the act.

They were now being beaten up. That they were still disease- enfeebled men, still hospital patients, evoked no response of a chivalrous or humanitarian nature in our captors. The cries con- tinued, on and off, all through the night and none of us slept. There was a terrible feeling of frustrated helplessness. In the guardroom our own men were being tortured and there wasn't a thing we could do about it. Any move or protest would only increase the rage and savagery of the guards.

Both the C.O. and the adjutant, who at least had some official recognition and were justified in attempting to intercede, went to the guardroom. The result of this action was that they, too, were beaten.

The next morning the dreaded Kempei-Tai, the Japanese secret police, moved in. We were ordered to leave our hut which was then searched from top to bottom. We were kept standing in the sun for several hours while this took place. Many of us were not very strong and this was quite an ordeal. At last the search of our hut was completed and we were permitted to return. We looked in dismay at what had been our clean, spruce ward. It had been literally ransacked. The Kempei-Tai had even ripped up boards in their search. We were not sure what they'd been searching for, probably just to see if there was any loot. Probably they didn't know themselves, because the Kempei-Tai seemed to have been selected for brutality rather than intelligence.

We set to work straightening things up and were getting things back to something like normal when there was another interruption. A party of Jap officers entered. They were in normal uniform but with them was the most evil-looking human I've ever seen. He wore a white straw hat, white shirt, white riding breeches and shining black top-boots. He had a revolver in a holster under his arm and he carried a stock whip which he twiddled in his hands and obviously wanted to use if given the slightest excuse.

The smartness of his dress was completely defeated by his posture, for he ambled like an ape. But if he was animal in this respect, his eyes, heavily lidded, were reptile.

Inevitably, someone murmured, "Gawd! The missing link." It wasn't much of an exaggeration. If this creature's picture had been included in a book on anthropology the casual reader would have glanced and accepted it as something akin to Neanderthal man.

We were informed he was the chief of the Kempei-Tai. He addressed us in broken English, difficult to follow because the accent was strongly American. But for the seriousness of the occasion – the fate of some of our own countrymen and the knowledge of the abominable savagery of which this creature was capable – the whole thing would have been laughable.

For all his menacing and evil appearance he was a travesty of an officer. He was the cartoonist's Jap military monster come to life. And his speech was a fantastic sequence of absurdities.

He declared that there was a sabotage ring operating against the Imperial Japanese Army in this area. There was strong suspicion that we officers were behind it. He made out that there was an underground military movement. And all this because a few men had acted foolishly and tried to flog some spades and so on.

They paid dearly for their folly. Apart from the beating up they were given the water treatment. This consisted of throwing the victim on his back, forcing a funnel into his mouth and pouring water down his throat until the utmost capacity was reached. His tormentors would then jump on him.

When they'd recovered from all this they were given a haircut, presented, for some illogical reason, with a bunch of bananas and taken away by the Kempei-Tai to Bangkok jail.

They were never seen or heard of again.

I tried to make inquiries after the war. I was told by some of our Intelligence people who were preparing the cases against certain Japanese war criminals that whenever prisoners were taken away by the Kempei-Tai there was no record of how, when, or where they were executed. Such unfortunates did, indeed, literally disappear.

Gradually life returned to the normal monotony, but many of us were not to stay much longer in this hospital camp. Some of the H 6 Force had been moved down from Tonchan to Tamarkand shortly after my own arrival. The rest of H 6 Force had pushed on. The survivors from this were eventually evacuated to Kanchanaburi Hospital Camp. And with them were many survivors from F Force.

News came that we were to join them. Apparently the Japanese High Command had ordained that as the railway was completed both F and H Forces should be rounded up, brought together and given some semblance of hospital treatment before being returned by the Siamese Imperial Japanese Army Command to the Singapore Command.

We'd gained sufficient strength for a move to Kanchanaburi to be feasible, so we gathered up our very meagre belongings. We were physically incapable of marching, so we were transported by native bus. It was a comparatively short run.

Outwardly, our new camp presented very much the same appearance as the one we'd just left. There was a different 'feel' about the place, because with the regrouping we were more members of the family rather than visitors.

Generally speaking, the food was better. It ran to an egg apiece for breakfast. These we mixed with the rice pulp. When eventually the H 6 survivors were brought together in one hut it resounded with the clatterings and whirrings of home-made egg whisks as we prepared our first meal of the day. Lunch remained bad, for it was restricted to rice. There was rice yet again for dinner, but embellished most evenings with a few chopped-up vegetables and even odd bits of meat.

Tamarkand Bridge Hospital Camp had been run by the Siam Command of the Japanese Army. Kanchanaburi belonged to the Malaya Command, from whom we'd been loaned. Perhaps our conditions improved because we had at last become somebody's responsibility. I think that being on loan accounted for some of the bad treatment we'd received when working on the railway. Siam Command had no real interest in us and we were no longer in an area administered by the command to which we belonged. Inevitably, in such a set-up, we were the ones who suffered wherever there were shortages. This, of course, applied to F Force even more so than ourselves.

We had no idea how the war was progressing. No news of any kind had reached us since we left Singapore. In part this was due to the impossibility of carrying wireless parts around with us. We didn't dare to try to obtain any, or improvise, because of the frightful stories of atrocities arising from the discovery of clandestine wireless sets in other camps.

In the light of subsequent knowledge I suspect very strongly that the Japanese attempts at belated hospital care were the result of the war no longer going in their favour. The prisoner-of-war casualties on the Thai–Burma railway were so appalling that even the Japs were becoming uncomfortable. The more far-sighted among them were worrying about how they could account for these should they lose the war. It was obvious, even to them, that an expression of regret and a confession that there had been mistakes would not be sufficient.

Certainly the Jap guards at Kanchanaburi were very mild and subdued in behaviour. I cannot recall a serious unpleasant incident. They tended to keep away from us. Contrary to what had been the rule at Tonchan and Tamarkand Bridge, we had a canteen where we could buy eggs and fruit from the Thais.

The Japanese officer who was in charge of the re-grouped survivors of H Force was a Lieutenant Terai. We'd first seen him when he arrived at Tamarkand to count and collect H 6 survivors. Perhaps rather curiously, we were all pleased to see him, even though we disbelieved his statements that we were to be moved to another hospital camp and then taken back to Singapore. It sounded too good. We knew, from bitter experience, that Japanese promises of better times to come had never been true.

At Kanchanaburi we saw Lieutenant Terai occasionally. He listened to our complaints and grievances. Sometimes he grinned. Always he did nothing about them. In his way he was friendly and he never displayed violence towards us.

Living conditions became more and more cramped as almost daily a fresh batch of living skeletons arrived. Many of these men were from F Force and their condition was pitiful beyond words.

By this time my own recovery was more satisfactory. John, the Australians and the American Merchant Navy officers were also up and about. We undertook what odd jobs we could, for the medical people were rushed off their feet. We were, after all, the strongest and fittest men in the new camp because we'd had the benefit of arriving at Tamarkand somewhat in advance of other survivors, and we'd enjoyed several weeks of convalescence.

One day I was roped in to help carry stretchers into the makeshift operating theatre. I seemed fated to have contact with the loathsome ulcer cases, for on this occasion the worst of them were being dealt with surgically. The patients were F Force survivors, so emaciated that they added little to the weight of the stretcher.

Our particular surgeon was an Australian, Dr Kevin Fagan, magnificent at his job. We brought in one patient and, after taking a careful look at him, we were told, "Take him back to the ward." This became an all-too-familiar formula. It meant that the poor sufferer was too near death for an operation to save him. The surgeons had to make some very difficult decisions indeed. In spite of all their skill so many of the sick had such little stamina left that post-operation shock killed them. What had to be remembered was that even without the operation they would have died anyway.

The shortage of vital supplies made the decisions all the more difficult. There were insufficient quantities of anaesthetics and sulphonamide. So every post-operation death meant a wastage of these, with the thought that someone else would probably die because they were not available for him.

In spite of my revulsion it was unavoidable, when helping the surgeons in even a menial way, that I should see something of the actual operations. I became accustomed to seeing the treatment of minor ulcers. They were cleared by spooning, which meant using a small scalpel shaped like a spoon. The black infected tissue was scooped away until bright red tissue was left. This was dusted with sulphonamide and bandaged.

But the day came when I saw a major operation; moreover, I had to help apply a tourniquet. The patient was a very bad shin ulcer case and the only hope was amputation. When I'd done all that was required of me I stood back, fascinated, watching the operation. It

119

was the cleanliness, the unhurried, orderly efficiency of the surgeon (Kevin Fagan), the anaesthetist (Dr Best) and the assistants which just filled me with admiration. It was little short of a miracle that they could maintain such a high-class standard with so little in the way of equipment and in such primitive surroundings. I didn't see the operation through to the very end. It was something of an ordeal to me and I was still comparatively weak. Waves of nausea started to overcome me and I was forced to go out as quickly as I could.

As I had noticed in the arrival ward at Tamarkand Bridge Camp it was at night that most of the deaths took place. As the hospital became more crowded with survivors from the railway the deaths naturally increased. It became necessary to arrange for a speedy removal of the corpses. An officer patrol was set up. Its job was to go quietly through the huts at night. At each one the wardmaster would report deaths and the patrol would silently gather up the bodies and place them outside, where they were covered with sackcloth.

The next day each was given a decent funeral with military honours. This seemed to appeal to the Japs, for they and the Korean guards turned out on every occasion that the funeral procession passed their guardroom. And slowly the Kanchanaburi cemetery filled. The sentiment was a bit trite but we really did have the feeling that this plot of land in Thailand had become a fragment of our own country.

We took it in turns to do the night patrol, so that most of us had only the one experience. For me the once was more than enough. It is a night I shall never forget. John was detailed to be with me and we spent most of the early part of the night on call. We sat in the cookhouse drinking black tea and keeping near the fire, for this was the time of year when the nights were getting colder.

We started on our grim round shortly after midnight. At each hut we reported to the wardmaster, who was usually a warrant officer. The removal of the dead was made easier by the fact that all the patients were on bamboo slats. Each body was lifted and quietly carried out. No word was spoken because we took every possible precaution to avoid waking those who were mercifully asleep. After the blanketed corpse was place under the eaves of the hut we'd go back with the wardmaster to collect the pitifully few personal belongings. These we took to Camp H.Q. where the duty officer sat by the light of a lantern.

We always brought in one identity disc; the other was left with the body. It was extraordinary how these never seemed to be lost. A man would come in wearing virtually nothing but a few rags, but his identity discs would be dangling from a string necklace.

Purely personal possessions, such as letters and papers, were retained by the duty officer and these were kept with the accompanying identity disc until the end of the war. Such things as clothing, boots, blankets and mess tins were put into store at H.Q. for re-issue to anyone who might be in need of them. And they were re-issued, because each day seemed to bring another batch of destitute, near-dead survivors.

Although I'd seen so much of death, I found this night a very harrowing one. There was not the nightmare ghastliness of that gathering up of the Tamil cholera corpses. This was something much more intimate, as though each body that I helped to carry from the wards was some close relative. It was impossible to think of the burden as just another corpse. I was too conscious that this had been a man, that somewhere a wife or a mother would mourn him, that he had come out east with a determination to do his bit, that he had faced the defeat, despair and degradation of the ghastly ordeals to follow. Now he was dead and I was carrying his body just a little nearer to its last resting place. It might so easily have happened the other way round. A feeling of brotherhood was created and as I staggered through the darkened wards with these pathetic dead I couldn't keep tears from my eyes.

Even in this camp, with its tragedies and its shocking revelations of what flesh and blood had had to endure, there were lighter, almost high-spirited, moments. There was no entertainment as such. We had to create what amusements we could. Our bodies were still too low and weary for anything energetic to be possible.

On our spare evenings we would sit outside the hut in the moonlight. I was, for some reason I could never understand, elected president of what we called "The Armchair Club". Needless to say, the armchairs were imaginary. I scratched around and persuaded or bullied various guests to talk about some pet interest or hobby. It wasn't easy to think up fresh items to provide a bit of novelty, and in the end I announced that the great honour of being president was so exacting that it was, I felt, time I resigned and made way for new blood. The Aussies, in particular, wouldn't hear of it.

I insisted and they, as they had threatened, sent me to a mock Coventry. The result was quite amusing. Members coming towards

121

me would suddenly about-turn and march briskly away. The game spread and it began to look as though I'd be cold-shouldered by everybody in camp. I capitulated. I resumed the exalted and onerous office and one of my first presidential acts was to tell them, with unpresidential rudeness, just what I thought of them. The Aussies, of course, found this terrifically entertaining. Instead of being apologetic they congratulated me on putting on a flaming good act.

Occasionally there was amusement from a situation which was in itself full of pathos. One night we received yet another group of half-dead human skeletons. Those who could walk were brought in for the nearest we could manage to a kitting up, as the Army calls it. We had nothing wonderful to offer, but these new arrivals were virtually destitute.

Out of the gloom and into the lantern-lit store strode an extraordinary looking figure. He was a stocky little man with long matted hair and a long black beard. His only garment was an old sack, tied like a kilt round his waist. His feet were wrapped in old rags tied with string. In his hands he had a rice bowl and a staff. Only his identity discs revealed that he was a British soldier and not an ancient Briton or a Neanderthal man.

In spite of his few rags, there was still something about his bearing which brought a tightening to our throat. There was a brief silence. Then somebody asked gently, "What kit do you need, laddie? What are you short of most?"

In a strong Scots accent – for it transpired he was one of the Jocks and a regular soldier – he said, "Give me the ruddy lot. I've got bugger all." There was something stout-hearted and defiant in his reply which, as well as the bluntness of his words, brought a ripple of laughter from the assembled officers.

Such was the quality of many of these men.

This was November 1943 and the nights were getting chillier. We, with our lowered resistance, felt the cold and started to light fires at night. However, this was quickly forbidden. The Japs, who administered the camp through our H.Q., objected to this as being too great a drain on the limited fuel supplies. This was not unreasonable because sufficient fuel for cooking was an ever-present problem.

The Thai nights at the end of the year can be decidedly cold, so it was as well for our comfort that we should suddenly receive orders which put us on the move again.

Our treatment at the hands of the Japs in this hospital camp was not too bad. We for our part took great care that there should not be any incidents, such as private excursions to the perimeter wire with the idea of trading or bartering. This was the secondary duty of the night patrols, performed in the intervals between bringing out the dead. I think we all dreaded another visit from the Kempei-Tai with their notorious savagery.

Of course, if they'd have let us have sufficient medical necessities more lives would have been saved. And while there was an improvement in rations we were certainly not getting the right food for building our wasted bodies up into a healthy condition.

As a personal example of how emaciated we were, my normal weight was in the region of 14 stone. At Tamarkand Bridge Camp, before I'd fully recovered from the ravages of fever, I was weighed and found to be 8 stone 10 lb. I think I must hold something of a record for tropical diseases. By the time I came to Tamarkand I'd suffered from beri-beri, pellagra, dengue fever, malaria, dysentery, blackwater fever, jaundice, scabies, ringworm, tropical ulcers, tropical pamphlicus (septic boils), and tinia (rash), double hernia, broken rib, one deformed testicle and intestinal parasites (whip worm).

But that period was now over and it seemed that the Japs were going to keep their promise that we should be returned to Singapore.

I look back on my time spent in Kanburi Camp with mixed feelings. Whereas at Tamarkand Bridge Camp I had been at death's door now, due to Philip Toosey and his staff, who had saved my life, I was faced with the long and slow process of gradually rebuilding it. Our main tasks were of a domestic nature, gathering firewood and helping the small medical staff to cope with the enormous job of tending the sick and disposing of the dead.

The Japs had decided that, as Tamarkand had been filled to capacity, now the influx of prisoners, in all degrees of illness, should be diverted to Kanburi. The railway had been completed at an enormous price in casualties. The empty trains coming down the line had been filled with the survivors from the jungle camps, plus all their dead. Most jungle camps had managed to cope with their dead as they happened by starting their own graveyards. It became apparent that, as the line was finished and the trains were empty, it would be more expedient to bring all and sundry down to Kanburi. The corpse patrol in Kanburi had managed to gather up the poor souls who died after they had arrived, but the main work now lay in the never-ending number who arrived dead.

123

Now it was the time for all fit and semi-fit to rally round the inadequate medical staff. An empty hut had been set aside and was known as the Mortuary. Here the dead were taken, were sewn up in a shroud of sacking and prepared for a decent funeral and a proper burial. Most of this work was carried out by the inmates of the camp who were fit enough to help.

Eventually a duty roster was made out, whereby it befell to the officers, as one would expect, to parade each day for funeral duties. They were ordered to put on a decent shirt, shorts and footwear wherever possible, and report outside camp H.Q. The funerals went on all day and every day, until the backlog had been completed. Someone had obtained a Union Jack and, after much arguing with the Jap guards, we were allowed to drape it over the body, which had been placed on a handcart. This was slowly escorted by two officers and one of the Padres down the lane to a large open piece of ground. This site was eventually taken over by the War Graves Commission after the war. From an open unkempt piece of land it became a most beautiful cemetery with flower beds and neat lawns. It was known worldwide for the number of British, Australian and Americans who lay there and became a focal point for visitors after the war.

The British graves were made up mostly of soldiers from the 18th Division (East Anglia) and contained men (among other Regiments) from the 4th, 5th & 6th Battalions of the Royal Norfolk Regiment.

There are no words or superlatives which can express my thoughts each time I carried out my duty. Here was a human being who had been reduced to the depths of degradation by another human being and it was hard to keep back the tears; it filled me with hatred and bitterness, which I still feel today. The dead had no Honours, Awards or Mention-in-Despatches. They had only done their duty, as ordered by their merciless captors. They had no option but to obey; defiance would mean either the firing squad or decapitation, such was the way of our captors who could beat and abuse those who had no way of standing up for themselves. I will always believe these men were killed by the enemy as much as if they had died on the battlefield. Of all the rotten jobs I had been forced to do, these funeral duties had the most profound effect on me mentally and in a way it was more harrowing than the physical effort of carrying tree trunks, burying dead Tamils suffering from cholera or the horror of having to live in the filth and squalor of the jungle railway camps.

The funeral ceremony was very simple and short, a few words from the Padre and some prayers; we had the satisfaction of giving them the honour and respect they so richly deserved. We had no music with which to sing the Hymn "Abide with Me", but it was recited as a prayer. In most cases the Padre concluded his words with "Abide with us O Lord, for it is towards evening and the day is far spent".

I often thought of the mentality of the Japanese High Command and the feasibility of building this God-forsaken railway. They hadn't the faintest idea of how to cope with thousands of unwanted prisoners. Perhaps they thought by sending most of them to build a railway through dense tropical jungle without proper food or medicines it would be a way of helping their wretched war effort and getting rid of a large number of unwanted prisoners at the same time. These two reasons alone, in contradiction of the Geneva Convention (which they signed but failed to ratify), would make their infamy doubly compounded.

After the war we learnt about our 2nd Battalion who had so heroically (with the rest of their Brigade) stopped the Japs at Kohima, the gateway to India. When the battle was over there, among the piles of Jap dead, were bodies whose leather belts had collections of British regimental badges, including our own Britannias, which had been taken during the Battle of Singapore.

After the war the Kanburi War Cemetery became the focal point of all those who paid homage and was visited by mothers, wives and relatives. I never went back, but one incident I read in the papers made me shed a tear. It said simply, "At one grave lay a large bunch of flowers with a note which bore the inscription 'To my beloved Son, Mother came to see you for Christmas'."

Finally the evacuation from the railway was completed. I consider it was brought about by the brilliant American Naval Victory at Midway. This was the turning point of the war in the Far East; it must have convinced the Japs at that time that they had lost the war, and they would no doubt have to face a terrible reckoning and retribution.

# Chapter 8

## RETURN TO SINGAPORE
## DECEMBER 1943–1944

The trains started taking us south. At first only the seriously ill and the medical staff left and they went direct to Changi where the main British prisoner-of-war hospital had somehow managed to keep going and where there were at least some facilities for coping with serious cases. I heard later that when the first truckloads of these poor wretches arrived from Singapore railway station the resident hospital and orderlies in Changi were appalled at the gruesome sight of the near-naked, wasted bodies which were brought to the Selerang parade square, where the hospital had moved from Roberts. Our people in the Changi area knew nothing of the railway, of the in-human treatment and of the frightful casualties. They'd imagined themselves to be losing weight badly and to be losing all their energy, but they were as fit men compared with these disease-ravaged skele-tons. One of the M.O.s told me later that he could scarcely believe his eyes.

The sufferers had to be lifted with the greatest care from the trucks, and carried gently into the hospital. Mercifully, many of them were not aware of what was happening.

But to return to Kanchanaburi. For ten days there was approxi-mately a train a day taking the survivors of F and H Forces. The worst cases, as I've said, went direct to Changi. The rest of us were taken to another camp in Singapore, at Syme Road.

As usual when we were on the move, the Japs managed to get us mixed up, though this time there was not nearly so much checking and rechecking. On this journey our Jap guards were much more humane in their treatment of us. It may have been because we were too ill and weakened to attempt escape or to give any trouble, or it may even have been that they were dismayed at having to move so many desperately ill men.

I found myself in charge of nineteen men from various regiments and corps. Both F and H Forces were represented. I knew none of them. There were the inevitable steel box trucks, but this time there was the luxury of straw bales. On the journey north there had been thirty to a truck, whereas now we were loaded on a basis of twenty, which again made for greater ease.

I looked anxiously at the men who had so suddenly become my responsibility. There were no high spirits. In fact there was no sound from them. Had I turned my back on them I wouldn't have been aware of their presence. I just hoped they'd survive the journey. I was no medical officer and I had nothing with me in the event of any becoming worse. There was only one medical officer for the whole train, so he could only be called on when we reached a halt.

It was possible to stretch out, and so I was able to get a fair amount of rest. In an odd way I enjoyed the journey, perhaps it was because we were on the move back to somewhere we knew to be a paradise compared with the hell we had left behind.

But the shadow of death was over us still. Shortly after we started we pulled up near a large junction called Pnom-pra-Duk. This was a night stop. None of my charges seemed to realize that anything had happened. We were permitted to keep the doors open and I knew John was in charge of a truck quite near to mine. I jumped down to the track and went in search of him. This was permitted because it was the usual custom at a halt for truck commanders to assemble for orders. It also provided the relief of a little gossip.

I found John, with some others, and we stood together watching the swaying lanterns of a party of men who were carrying someone from the train. An officer and the medical officer were with them.

I wondered how many more would not manage to finish this journey.

The dead man was buried somewhere near the track. I don't know how the grave was marked. It was a fact, though, that when the War Graves Commission came to Siam they did an almost miraculous job in discovering where our dead were buried, even recovering bodies from the Burma frontier. These corpses were eventually brought together and reburied in Kanchanaburi Cemetery, where already so many Force F and H bodies rested.

These tragic halts for burials marked our southward train journey. Always the train was stopped and the Japs waited patiently. They seemed anxious that the dead should receive the correct respect. If only they could have had a fraction of this consideration for the living over the previous months!

The behaviour of the Japs was often quite unpredictable. For coolness we had the truck doors open and one luckless fellow fell out during the night. It transpired later that he wandered around and eventually gave himself up when he found a Jap military post. Instead of being killed instantly as an escapee, he was treated with absolute hospitality and completed his journey to Singapore with an escort – in a passenger train!

In general, though, the Jap attitude towards us was undergoing a great change. Perhaps their higher-ups realized the inevitable result of the war. The Siam–Burma railway and the treatment of the prisoners-of-war who had been forced to labour on it were sure to be the subject of awkward questions at a peace conference. The casualty and sickness figures were too high to be explained away. Whatever the reason, not only was our treatment better but everything was done in a more leisurely manner. Whenever the train stopped, the men, those at least who were well enough to move, were permitted to climb down from the trucks and sit on the platform or embankment. When it was time to move on the Jap sentries shepherded them back and there were no face-slappings or ear-boxings. Not even excited abuse.

Watching all this I felt stirrings of hope. Perhaps the worst was over.

There was also an improvement in our rations. On the way north the issue had been one cupful of boiled rice three times a day, plus a cup of black tea. Returning, we had some stewed vegetables and either a bit of fish or meat thrown in.

We were able to add to this, because at the various halts the local people, both in Siam and Malaya, were allowed to approach the train unhindered. We were able to buy a few extras from them. They chatted and seemed friendly, in fact, more friendly than ever before. This may have been because the Japs were not harassing, or because they felt very sorry for us. And at the back of it there was the undeniable fact that the much-publicized Greater East-Asia Co-prosperity Sphere had proved a complete flop.

The Bangkok Express provided a most amazing contrast as it moved past us one night. We'd halted at a wayside station and it pulled in, slowing down. From the open door of my wagon I could see into the dining-car. It stopped right opposite me. I could see the brightly-lit interior. There were white tablecloths and table lamps and white-jacketed waiters. There were civilians, wealthy Thais most probably. There was one very beautiful Malay girl who looked straight at me. Although there were Jap officers in the diner, she smiled and waved. The memory of that warmed me for quite a long time.

There was, however, an extraordinary incident yet to come. The express started to pull out. A waiter appeared, leaned out and threw us a packet of dinner rolls, at the same time singing "God Save the King".

This incident came back to me very forcibly a few years later. I was travelling with a party of troops in a military train running through Germany and Austria. I was in a first-class compartment with some bars of chocolate, fruits and other luxuries.

In the evening we pulled up at a small station in Austria. A group of little children came trotting along past the train. They looked pinched. They were begging for food. I had a sudden memory of that other train journey and the packet of rolls. I opened the window and threw out everything I had to the eager youngsters.

The troops were doing the same, though I believe it was against orders. But I wasn't thinking of orders; I was remembering. I hope we looked as pleased and grateful to that waiter as these little children did to us.

To return to our journey south. We stopped in Kuala Lumpur. Here I joined John on the platform and we strolled to and fro. We bought pineapples and even had an ice cream. As I'd already had dysentery I felt there was no great risk, but the M.O. was annoyed and assured us there were probably other bugs in it which we hadn't had yet. I told him I didn't think this was possible. I'd had the lot.

Eventually we reached Singapore. There were lorries waiting for us. These were driven by our own people, men who'd been retained in Singapore as drivers and so had escaped the fate which had befallen so many of us. The troops climbed or were helped into the back of the lorry. Officers went up front with the driver.

We were to be taken to Syme Road Camp. It was a night drive and my first impression was how smooth the going was compared with the roads of Siam. There was, too, an impression of freshness and cleanness, and I marvelled at the street lamps as a child would at an illuminated Christmas tree.

I chatted with my driver. He felt they'd had a bad time in Singapore lately. The rice ration had been reduced and there were fewer perks. The black market wasn't so good either. There were definitely fewer tins of bully and other commodities. I was secretly amused.

The streets were well lit and I could see that the bomb rubble had been cleared up. It all looked so wonderful that I kept staring. It was the return to the world from purgatory.

The driver knew something of our hardships. "My Gawd!" he said, "when I saw the first lot of your blokes arrive! I was taking 'em to hospital and I was worried stiff they'd all die before I could get 'em there." His present passengers, he thought, looked pretty bad, to say the least of it.

He told me that we'd be all right at Syme Road. It was a camp in the open country part of Singapore Island, next to a golf course. It was a hutted camp, with showers, lights, proper roads. It sounded like a paradise to me.

And Syme Road Camp turned out to be everything the driver had claimed. As we climbed down from the trucks we were received by the Senior British Officer and the camp H.Q. staff. There were only a few Japs present.

I was surprised to discover that the camp H.Q. personnel were actually the fittest of the F and H Force survivors. They'd been brought down in advance to organize the camp for our arrival. The change in their appearance, after only a few days of civilization, was amazing. They were clean and well shaven. Their footwear was polished. Shirts, shorts or slacks, all were clean. Officers and W.O.s wore polished badges of rank. Even more like finding myself back into the past, I saw the once-familiar armbands of the adjutant and the quartermaster. It was all a rather bewildering experience.

We were treated very kindly. I handed over my poor, long-suffering group of nineteen men. They were taken off into the night towards one of the huts. I sat on my old pack, watching them marching off in their rags and tatters, and with their black beards and all. I was not to know it then, but this was the last time for the duration of the war that I should actually command a party of British troops.

From now until peace was signed the Japs started to segregate nearly ninety per cent of the officers to run their own part of the camps, including all the fatigues, the kitchen work and the gardening.

When all the men had been taken away for the night, John and I in company with the other 'truck commanders' were shown to the officers' lines. Our guide showed us into a dry, well-lit wooden hut with a concrete floor – and apologized for the spartan conditions.

We quickly had our bedrolls down and fell fast asleep on the floor. No doubt it was a hard bed, but it was the best night's sleep we had had for a very long time, perhaps because of the greater ease of mind. After what we had experienced we could never feel free from tension so long as we were still near the accursed railway. There was always the thought of being dragged back, and, in the damp jungle, with its perpetual odour of decay, there was no deep peace of mind.

The worst must be over. We'd come through. We slept.

With morning the transformation in our appearance from wild men of the woods to civilized beings took place. The whole time was devoted to cleaning ourselves under the showers and washing our belongings. I must have stayed under the shower for at least half an hour. It was my first bath since that April day when we'd bathed in the river just outside Bampong on our way up to the railway. And this time there was soap. We'd been issued with some, and with razor blades by the camp H.Q.

Some officers took their clothing into the shower and washed the garments, beating them on the concrete floor of the shower bath.

It was an order that all beards had to go. In addition to the issue of blades there was a camp barber in attendance. He was a cheery Australian named Clarry Tremalyn. I remembered him from Kanchanaburi where he used to go round shaving some of the very sick. Now he appeared all ready to cut hair and to shave off beards, using a cut-throat razor.

It was wonderful to be rid of matted hair and beards, together with the parasites which infested them.

John and I spent the rest of the day boiling up our clothes and blankets in buckets. The amount of dirt that came out was astonishing; dead bugs, lice and other vermin floated to the top. The dead lice looked exactly like miniature shrimps.

We dried the cleaned garments quickly in the afternoon sun. After the filthiness of our general appearance and condition, the urge for cleanliness was great and the camp was well organized to provide this.

The camp staff set an example of smartness with armbands, polished buttons and cap badges. There were inevitable cracks about 'bags of bull', but I felt it was good for us. We'd satisfied our need for a clean-up, but it required a little effort to avoid lapsing back into more slipshod ways.

It was good, too, to have a smoothly-running camp after the chaos of so many of the places we'd been in since we'd left Singapore.

After a few days at Syme Road we were told that a high Japanese officer was coming to see us and talk to us. The Japs had a notice board and there was an announcement to this effect. It provoked derisive comment. Someone said, "He couldn't be any higher than we were when we arrived from Siam."

It was decided, though, to put on a very carefully planned show for the General. All the thinnest men, those who still bore marked traces of starvation, were to be in the front rows. They were to wear their oldest and most ragged uniforms, but it was essential that they should be absolutely clean. It was important to give the impression that we were doing our best under the poor conditions we had been forced to endure. To have paraded a crowd of scruffy, bearded hooligans in jock straps and with rubber tyres on their feet wouldn't help us. It would be regarded, rightly, as an insult.

Relations between us and the Japs at this camp were fairly reasonable. We were enclosed by a high barbed-wire fence which was occasionally patrolled by a Jap sentry. There was the usual Jap guard-room at the main gate and they also had a large house there.

The Jap commandant was a lieutenant named Takahashi and he was eventually given command of the Changi area. Takahashi was, to use the troops' expression, "a good Nip". Under his administration there were no ugly incidents or outrages. After the war several ex-prisoners gave evidence on his behalf when he was on trial for war crimes.

While I was at Syme Road the British officer in charge was Lieutenant-Colonel Newey of the Malayan Volunteers. In point of fact he was not the most senior officer, but he'd worked before with Takahashi and they seemed to have reached a reasonable understanding.

I've heard criticisms that our camp H.Q. tended to be "Jap happy", but I think these were unjustified. Although only the F and H Forces survivors who were in the best physical shape were sent to this place, it was still virtually a hospital camp. Compared with the death rolls up in Siam or at Kanchanaburi our mortality rate was low, although there were daily deaths. But for those other truly appalling figures,

132

ours would have been regarded as outrageous. In circumstances such as these even the most trivial concession was valuable and it was worth bending over backwards in order to keep our Jap captors good-tempered towards us. With so many men's lives in so precarious a state the responsibility must have weighed very heavily on our own camp H.Q. I think it was because of this enormous strain that, as time went on, there was a succession of Senior British Officers. It was too much for one man to endure over a lengthy period.

The result, anyway, of an 'appeasement' policy was that we were in a well-run camp, with conditions as comfortable as possible.

The day of the great parade arrived. We were assembled according to plan. The thinnest men in the oldest clothes were placed in the front ranks. The healthiest and best-dressed were at the back. My own place was somewhere in the middle.

Lieutenant Takahashi opened the proceedings and introduced the 'high Japanese officer'. He was, in fact, General Saito. He was in charge of all the prisoners taken in Malaya and no doubt was largely responsible for arranging our return from Siam. He was a plump, heavily-built man with heavy jowls and a small black moustache. When years later I saw the film *The Bridge Over The River Kwai* the Japanese colonel in the film reminded me vaguely of General Saito. In the film I thought the Jap, as played by Sessue Hayakawa, was far too nice for the part.

General Saito addressed us through the medium of an interpreter. His manner was restrained and he didn't bark his words out. He appeared to be moved by what he had heard of our ordeal and heavy losses. There was a report, at the end of hostilities, that he committed hari-kari. Perhaps, when he spoke to us, he'd already decided that his own days were numbered. It would account for his manner. The interpreter had to use pidgin English. I still remember his words: "High Japanese officer is not happy – there is so much ill health and absolutely no faith left in Japanese. You must get healthy [he pronounced it 'hellshee'] again. He will do what he can do!"

The General and his retinue, including the interpreter, departed and we were dismissed.

The general impression among us was that Saito had been sincere but we wanted some action, not words. We'd been through too much for a few sympathetic words to make any difference. Most of us doubted whether anything would be done, so we were delighted when our rations were increased. We were given soya beans with every rice issue, and occasionally there were tit-bits. Some men disliked soya beans. I enjoyed them and obtained more by trading my rice.

The Dutch officers discovered a way of making something approaching a fermented cream cheese from soya beans. They called it Tempi. The process was primitive. It was fermented in an old bath and it had to be pounded by jumping up and down in it with bare feet. This ritual amused us all, particularly the Diggers. It was the Old Timer's favourite joke to come into the hut and say to me, "Reg – I've put you down for Tempi-stamping fatigue." Using his own language and exaggerating his accent I'd reply, "Turn it up, Bert!"

Another improvement was that we received pay regularly: thirty Japanese Malay dollars a month. We were able to spend this in the camp canteen on coconuts and pineapples.

Life was comparatively pleasant here and the majority of us regained a modicum of health. Instead of being more or less at death's door we were restored to the low level of health which we'd known before our move to Siam. It was a minimum level at which the prisoners who remained in Singapore had managed to keep themselves.

The death rate dropped. A great number of the men were so weak that they had to be excused duty and for the fittest among us the best we could manage was to deal with our essential chores, with a little extra exertion occasionally on such projects as making Tempi.

Most of the tropical diseases gradually cleared up, including my own malaria. The jungle sores, ulcers, and other skin complaints lingered stubbornly. The only available treatment was nearly as bad as the complaint. Daily we were shepherded to the Camp Skin Centre. This sounds impressive, but what happened was that we were each given an old tin filled with boiling water, some lint and a measure of a solution called Eusol. This was a compound of chloride intended for purifying drinking water. However, as it was a disinfectant and the only one in abundance we were compelled to use it for skin infection.

Each patient had to treat himself and it was sheer agony to dab ringworm and other sores with this mixture of boiling water and Eusol. I had four skin complaints – small ulcers, ringworm, scabies and tropical pamphlicus. Using the prescribed treatment, it took me six months to get rid of my troubles.

We kept up our spirits by joking about the Skin Centre. It was regarded as inevitable that if you went there with one skin disease they'd discover another one. It was slanderously suggested that the centre was a place where you became infected with another disease.

I was comparatively fortunate that my skin trouble was mostly on the arms and lower legs. Some unlucky men had infection between the legs and this made walking a torture. They used to go around wearing nothing but boots or rubber tyre footwear, and something in the nature of a g-string. To avoid friction they had to walk bow-legged and, in spite of sympathy for them, it was often hard to keep back laughter, for they looked like a bunch of cow-punchers.

We did have a hospital in Syme Road Camp and our most seriously ill men were accommodated there. Gradually those patients who survived were discharged and joined the rest of us in the general huts.

Few of us could even remember when we'd last seen an entertainment, so there was much enthusiasm when we started a camp concert party. There was a search for talent. I tried my hand at writing sketches. One was a frivolity about a French family, the other a spy-drama burlesque. In each I acted and achieved stardom overnight, only to lose the exalted position just as quickly. John was given the job of wardrobe master and also helped me in the production of my sketches.

I think I owed my theatrical success to the Australians in the audience, and an ex-pugilist from my regiment, who rejoiced in the name of "Slogger" Harrington. For a small consideration he would sit in the centre of the audience and applaud violently whenever I came on the stage. His fists were large and powerful and as they came together while clapping it sounded like the crack of doom; but it managed to set off the rest of the audience to do likewise. The Diggers excelled themselves at side-splitting interruptions and general barracking. There were moments, in fact, when actors and audience seemed to change roles, and many a line being delivered from the stage was broken because the actor became convulsed with laughter.

Our costumes and props were miracles of inventiveness. We even had top hats, made from blackened cardboard, and opera cloaks which were Dutch Army groundsheets dyed black.

One of the Australians was in the cast of my French sketch. He was a very tall man named Lew Martin. He'd been with a different party of H Force, but had joined up with our Diggers at Kanchanaburi. In the part of Papa Dupont (the Blasé Roué) he had to wear very tight pantaloons and when he appeared on the stage there was a great deal of earthy and bawdy comment from the audience. Fortunately there were no ladies present, but some of the remarks would have made even a brewer's mate blush.

My own entrance (as the son – Merchant Edouard), through the audience carrying a bunch of flowers, brought about more applause and catcalls, and when I joined Lew on the stage it was several minutes before we could get started.

My first concert party was an enormous success. It was succeeded by others. There was a queue of would-be actors and so, for the time being, I lapsed into obscurity. The Diggers liked to walk past me saying loudly, "I wonder what happened to the comedian joker in that French sketch." There was even an unkind suggestion that I'd pinched the box-office money and cleared out.

The tall Australian caused an incident which, in any other camp, might have resulted in tragedy. He went out one night, quite near the barbed wire, rehearsing his lines. The Jap guards pounced on him and dragged him off to the guardrooms. In order to show just what he'd been doing, he had to go through his lines again, this time before the stony-faced Jap guard commander, who, no doubt, couldn't understand a word. Somehow he managed to convince the Japs that in shouting and waving his arms about he had not been signalling to anyone outside the camp and he was released.

It was a long time before he heard the last of this incident, which must have been one of the funniest performances ever given. His fellow Diggers certainly rubbed it in. I heard one say, "Well done, Lew. A command performance – perhaps they'll ask you to appear before Tenno-Heiko [the Jap Emperor] in *Madame Butterfly*." "Were you rehearsing Lew – or acting a part?"

We celebrated Christmas at Syme Road. We had a church service but supplies were too meagre for there to be anything in the way of a Christmas dinner. However, one great luxury did appear along with our rice and soya beans – two spoonfuls of white sugar! But there was little else because we were not so well organized in our earliest days at this camp, and our strength was much too wavery. We had, at this time, just started the concert party – it was before my first contribution – and they managed to put on a panto. I think the most outstanding feature of this show was the decor, which was the work of Ronnie Searle.

From Christmas onwards news of the war began to filter through to us. We'd been ten months without hearing anything apart from vague rumours. We had neither the materials nor the opportunities to make a radio at Syme Road, but news was brought to us from the Changi area by drivers of the sick trucks. They also smuggled in local mail.

It was from this source that we learnt that Italy had capitulated. We didn't get the full story, so we had no idea there'd been any choice, or that some of the Fascists were still fighting on the side of the Germans. It so happened that at the time the King of Italy broadcast to his people telling them to surrender to the Allies there were two Italian submarines in Singapore harbour. Before they could slip away the Japs boarded them and took the crews prisoner.

Our camp H.Q. issued an announcement that certain Italian officers would be arriving shortly. One hut was wired off and some screens were erected. The prisoners were installed in this, in quarantine virtually. For a few weeks we were not allowed to go anywhere near them, but at last the day came when they were turned loose. We had been told, by this time, that they had had a choice and that they were with us because they'd obeyed their sovereign instead of Hitler, Mussolini and Tojo. It took a bit of accepting that they were now on our side, but our mistrust broke down quite quickly. For their part they were very shy and certainly behaved entirely circumspectly. I think it was to their credit that not a solitary member of the crews of these two submarines avoided imprisonment by opting to fight on with the Japs.

So we accepted these Italian officers into the brotherhood of Allied prisoners-of-war. John and I became quite friendly with two of them, a Commander and a Lieutenant. The lieutenant, whose name was Rafaeli Papa, appeared to be quite a ladies' man. He prided himself on this and had a select collection of photographs of truly glamorous girls. He passed these round the hut. It was one of the strangenesses of the war that this man, now sharing imprisonment with me, had been on leave in Paris in August 1943 and gone to the Folies Bergère while I was nearly dying of blackwater fever in Tamarkand Camp. Would either of us, given a glimpse of the other, have believed that our paths would cross?

Bert, the Old Timer, was soon pulling the legs of the Italians, particularly Rafaeli's. "Know why those Sheilas all fell for you, Rafaeli?" he asked.

"No, Signor Bert. Why?"

"Because we were all locked up, cobber. No competition. Only you dagoes and huns running around in Paris. No Diggers!"

One of the other Australians looked very critically at Bert and then exclaimed, "Stone the crows! You're no lady-killer, Bert." Bert pretended to be deeply offended.

In the centre of the camp we had a little café called The Flying Dutchman. It was run by our camp H.Q. as an officers' café. Most nights we gathered here and sat talking over a cup of coffee. The coffee was made by the staff, Dutch other ranks, from rice which was toasted. It wasn't at all bad. There were also "camp doovers". These were rice biscuits. We could also get rice cakes and soya bean sandwiches. The charges were very modest, a few cents, which went towards the central messing fund.

The café was very popular and was particularly crowded after one of the camp shows had been put on. The "actors" frequented it and the place became a social centre. It was the scene of a quite dramatic incident one evening.

The usual talk was in progress when suddenly a Korean guard, obviously drunk, staggered in. He lurched to an empty table, flopped down and started to bang with his fists, shouting, "Coffee! Coffee! Kurrah!" In spite of his drunken condition he looked fierce and he had his rifle with him, the bayonet fixed. The waiters were too scared to move.

All conversation died down and there was only the shouting of the Korean. One of the officers present stood up, crossed to the bar and then took a cup of coffee to the Korean. The Korean solemnly thanked him.

We were wondering what this meant. Was the man genuinely drunk, or was he pretending?

The Korean suddenly exclaimed, "Nippon soon finish war. She no goodega! All over! You go home Ingrisu. Churchill Number One – very goodega."

We were amazed. There was the possibility the man might be a plant, trying to find out what we knew. If so, he learnt nothing. There was silence. Only the officer who'd taken him the coffee spoke. He just said, "Ah! So."

The Korean drained his coffee in one gulp, staggered to his feet, gripped his rifle firmly and lurched out into the night. There was quite a silence. Then in lowered voices we discussed what had just happened. Was it a straw in the wind?

I was remembering a time in Tanjong Rhu when a drunken guard had boasted, "You go Tokyo in chains. I go London. I sleep with your girl." I think the sight of this particular near-baboon would have made any English girl pass out.

But what a contrast between these two incidents! This one certainly raised our spirits, but they were quickly to be cast down because word came that we were due for another move, this time to Changi, where we would be housed in the jail. This depressed us greatly, for we knew that that inhospitable building could only offer us cells and court-yards. It might be an end to strolling and sitting in the sun, to social life, to visits between old friends. It was bad enough to be within the confines of a camp, but this prospect was of walls closing in upon us.

Our depression, however, didn't prevent a few attempts at jokes. I said to the Old Timer, "I knew you jokers would finish up in 'jile' but I didn't think I'd have to go with you."

Bert's look of injured innocence was masterly. "It's you pommie bastards who should go to 'jile' – not us poor, honest Diggers."

I exclaimed, "Listen to one of the old Botany Bay convicts talking! You can still see the handcuff marks on his wrists."

This produced loud laughter from everyone except Bert, who protested, "Oh, break it down!"

The Changi rumour proved only too true. The Japs erected large screens round some of the huts which were cleared of occupants. One day an open lorry arrived and we had a tantalizingly quick glimpse of white women. They were civilian internees who were just being moved from the jail, which had been their place of incarceration.

A quick wave and they were gone from our sight. These were the first white women I had seen since the day I disembarked in Singapore.

This incident cheered us up. We felt that if women and children had lived in Changi jail we should be able to survive.

The trucks which had brought them were driven to our side of the camp. With resignation we started to load up our few belongings. We were counted, and re-counted, and then we were driven along familiar roads to the familiar area of Changi.

We went to jail quite cheerfully, sitting on our kit. My nearest companions in the truck were John Hayne and Adrian Davies. Davies was known as Ack. He was a Welshman with a quiet sense of humour and the three of us got along very well together. Ack was popular with the Australians. They tended to regard him as one of themselves and he often reminded them: "I come from Wales, not New South Wiles." The Old Timer said, "Funny thing, Ack, we knew you weren't a pommie but we didn't realize you were an abo from the outback of Wiles."

We were driven at moderate speed and I thought of the breakneck journey in January 1942 when I'd had my first sight of Changi jail, never dreaming that I would one day become an inmate. It was now April 1944, but there'd been so much suffering and hardship that the interval seemed more like ten years.

Changi Jail is heavily fortified. There is a high outer wall and an inner one not quite so high. We were driven into this chasm of concrete. It was a very hot morning and the walls on either side of us seemed to cut off all the air. We clambered down from our trucks and unloaded our 'luggage'. I could barely manage to lift my bundle of rags down from the tailboard of the lorry and some of my companions hadn't even the strength to do this unaided. It reveals the general physical condition of the Siam railway survivors, because we were regarded as being 'fit'.

Changi jail was already occupied by Allied prisoners-of-war and many of them watched from a distance as we gathered between the walls and settled down on our bundles waiting for the Japanese. It was a long wait, trying in the intense, concentrated heat.

"Look up there," John said.

He indicated one of the corners. There was a little glassed-in sentry-box with a searchlight and a machine gun. There was a Jap sentry looking down on us. The other corners of the walls had a similar guard-post. They were a grim reminder of our status.

I don't know where or how it started, but there was soon a rumour circulating that our stay inside the jail would only be brief because the Nips were constructing an officers' camp just outside the walls. For once rumour turned out to be true, but most of us didn't believe it at the time.

At last our long wait in the sun came to an end. The official Japanese welcoming party arrived. There was a soap-box which was placed in position and a dapper officer mounted this and postured, his Samurai sword much in evidence. Around him stood an interpreter and an assorted collection of what we took to be 'yes-men'. To complete the party there was a little man with an abacus. It was fantastic to see this kindergarten adding-up device used by grown men of the Imperial Japanese Army.

We were ordered to stand up. The man with the abacus worked feverishly as we were counted, and re-counted, and counted again.

This procedure always struck me as lunatic. What did it matter if they lost one wretched half-starved officer? They'd lost men by the thousand up in Siam, through starvation and neglect. Their overall record of prisoners-of-war could never be accurate.

At last the pantomime of efficiency was over and the next stage of the proceedings started. This was a typical harangue from the officer on the soap-box. It began by the interpreter announcing, "This man – he say he is the boss." This solemnly-intended introduction sparked off roars of applause from the prisoners and order was not restored until there was some ear-boxing here and there.

The speech went on and on. I suppose it was meant to impress us, though it was rather a fiasco afterwards because we never saw the 'boss officer' again. His place was taken by Lieutenant Takahashi from Syme Road, whom we almost regarded as a friend.

Finally, a long argument developed between the Jap 'boss' and our senior officers. This was over the roll. The interpreter outlined the categories.

"How many men fit."

"How many men sick."

"How many men fit for work."

"How many men sick can work."

"How many men sick no work."

It just went on and on and my attention wandered. I turned to the Old Timer who was standing just behind me.

"What's he saying now, Bert?" I asked.

Without hesitation the reply came in an excellent imitation of the interpreter: "This man – he say how many men tunnelling."

Bert didn't keep his voice down and there was an immediate gust of laughter. It was infectious and soon there was complete chaos. The parade was right out of hand. The Japs were bewildered at first. They seemed to argue a bit among themselves. Then they became angry and there was some face-slapping. At last order was restored, though tears were streaming down my cheeks as I struggled to keep down my laughter and I was far from being the only one in difficulties. The cause of all the trouble, the Old Timer, looked blankly innocent.

Nearly all the morning had been wasted in waiting and the pointless reception ceremony. We were at last allocated our quarters inside the jail. The jail itself was roughly in the shape of a capital H, with grass courtyards and administrative buildings between the prison blocks. These main blocks consisted of rows of cells on three floors, connected by iron stairways. There were metal grilles underfoot and there was a frightful clatter as men moved around the block.

We were placed four officers in a small cell which normally housed one convict. In each cell corner was an Asiatic squatter latrine, namely just a small oval hole in the concrete, with a pedal for flushing; strict orders were issued that they were never to be used under any circumstances owing to the overcrowding and health hazards involved. Instead latrines were dug in the grass area in the exercise yard. One ingenious Sapper officer constructed a urinal by placing an old gramophone horn upside down on a pipe dug into the ground leading to a soak-away. This was humorously referred to as the Pissaphone. It always provoked laughter when referred to, especially when one chap said he'd like to see his mother-in-law sitting on it.

In truth the jail was quite modern. John, Ack and I were allocated a cell in E block. It had a concrete plinth and headrest and there was a squatter latrine in the corner. Standing on the slab of cement in the middle of the cell it was possible to touch each wall by stretching out the arms. There was a large steel door with sliding mechanism. A small grille admitted air. There was a socket for an electric light bulb, but no cell given to us had the luxury of a bulb. The dimensions of our cell was approximately 6 feet by 10 feet, and one realized what it must have been like to have been locked up in the Black Hole of Calcutta.

Many Asiatic prisoners, living in squalor, would have found these cells almost luxury accommodation, but with three officers to a cell we were uncomfortably overcrowded.

When night came, John slept on the slab, while I slept down the side away from the latrine. Ack lay the other way across our feet. I say "slept", but this was what none of us succeeded in doing. We were much too cramped and I, for one, experienced the sheer terror of claustrophobia. Some officers were less fortunate than we were and had to sleep four to a cell. I can't imagine how they managed.

However, even in all this discomfort, the Australians managed to provide some fun. Just before their door clamped shut they put out their clogs and old boots. For cleaning, they explained, by the Nip hotel staff.

We'd received strict orders that on no account were we to make use of the Asiatic squatter latrines. The water was cut off to avoid serious risk of pestilence. At least they provided us with a bit of amusement. One officer was heard to complain, "Ruddy funny wash hand-basin – right down in the floor." Another went around complaining that when he wanted a wash he couldn't get his head into it although he could get his tooth mug in.

There was, in general, so little to laugh about that even a below-average joke achieved success.

What did amuse us all was that the Australians had been bunched together in a much larger room, rectangular in shape. From its penal use it was known as the Flogging Room. In military slang it seemed most appropriate they should have been put there, because in point of fact they were flogging everything they could lay their hands on!

It was a fact that they were almost immediately 'in business'. I dropped in to have a chat with them and I was grumbling about having to sit in the dark once we were locked in our cells. The Old Timer said he reckoned he could get us a bulb. The price was agreed and he promised delivery the next day. I paid and he kept his word, but we were cheated out of our light because when we tried the bulb we found it had a broken filament.

The following day I tackled the Old Timer. He said at once, "Sorry, cobber. I'll get you a good one."

He did. It was an exceedingly good bulb and we enjoyed its light even more when we discovered that it had been fiddled from the office of the Jap commandant, Lieutenant Takahashi himself. Just how it had been done we never knew. The Diggers never gave away 'trade secrets'. They provided us with other small luxuries, the odd blanket, a plate, a few cheroots.

There were many complaints about the cramped quarters for sleeping and permission was granted for us to sleep in the courtyard. It was heavenly to breathe fresh air and to feel comparatively free.

We did what we could to brighten up our dreary cells. A few faded, well-thumbed pin-ups emerged. We were beginning to settle down and make the best of things when we were moved once more. This was a temporary move, to ease the overcrowding inside the jail. We marched out of the prison and up the road to Selerang Square. It was not a great distance. This was the very square where we had assembled for the start of our journey to the "holiday camps in the Malayan hills" which had turned out to be the horror camps along the Siam–Burma railway.

Some of the friends who had seen us off were here to meet us. It was exciting, as we marched into the square, to look at the men who were waiting for us, to pick out old friends. And as soon as we were dismissed we broke up into little groups, talking eagerly. One of the first to come up to me was my tall friend from the Suffolks, Donald Wise. I had last seen him after the march into Kanchanaburi. He'd awakened me when I'd fallen asleep in the full heat of the midday sun.

In civilian life he had been a newspaper reporter. Incidentally, he still follows that calling. True to his profession he had a fund of information. He had not fared so badly as many of us, because he'd been kept in Kanchanaburi until his return to Singapore.

Although I heard some dreadful stories from F Force survivors at Tamarkand and Kanchanaburi and was prepared for horrors, some of the news Donald gave me shocked me.

The very worst cases were from the most advanced camps up the railway line. Because of their distance from base, these survivors were among the last to be brought out. This happened while my own party and other groups were recovering from the worst of our illnesses in Tamarkand and Kanchanaburi.

Our medical officers were convinced that these poor fellows should have been given some sort of medical care as quickly as possible instead of being subjected to an appallingly long journey. The Japs, however, were feverishly impatient to get them right away from the railway as fast as possible. They did this against the recommendations of our medical people. Perhaps they were horrified at the casualty figures, in view of the way the war was going, and were most anxious there should be no more deaths in the railway area. The only argument in favour of their decision was that these men were so ill they needed the very best hospital treatment possible and this, due to restrictions on medical supplies, was Selerang in the Changi area.

Donald told me that the shambles when the trucks bringing these F Force victims from the railway station arrived was past description. The sick men had to be carried into the hospital and they were so fragile it was a wonder they didn't fall apart. They'd had virtually no treatment on the way down and were all in a truly revolting condition.

It seems the true casualty figures will never be known, but the country alongside the railway from Kanchanaburi to Three Pagodas Pass and on into Burma was littered with Allied graves. It's said that approximately six out of every ten men sent there failed to return. As for the railway, it proved of little use to the Japs because it was quickly put out of action by Allied bombers.

144

After I'd talked with Donald I moved on and I was greeted by Eric Prattley, the C.O. of the 5th Royal Norfolks. It was grand to see him again. It seemed to help to restore a sense of sanity, especially as we talked of the days before the war and recalled how, when I was a very green second lieutenant, he'd given me encouragement for the ordeal of meeting 'Jumbo' Wilson, who was then our divisional commander.

Most of the people who met us on this day had remained in the Changi area all the time. To us they looked wonderfully healthy and strong. But in normal times I imagine every one of them would have been rushed away to a convalescent home to spend a few months recuperating. Their basic diet had been much as ours, though they had not had to do hard labour on it. And the Changi area was always a good place for augmenting rations. The surrounding land was fertile and there were many gardens. There were also coconut and banana trees and pineapple plants.

There was a canteen in the area, so to us it was rather like a return to a land of plenty. Our sleeping quarters were in a bombed house. This was for a very short time; before we could even start to get organized we were moved back to the walls of the jail.

The other ranks were still accommodated in the jail. Officers were quartered where the jail employees had once lived. These were the coolie lines. Each line consisted of an atap hut; then a long, low concrete building with little rooms, each with its own verandah, and finally another atap hut. These composite lines were lettered from A to I. At first I was put in F2 with two other captains. This was the concrete building in composite line F.

We had a living-room, a small kitchen behind it, and a latrine in the corner of that. And while we lived where the labourers had lived, our Jap guards occupied the prison warders' houses.

John was in one of the atap huts, where several of our friends were, and, as soon as I could manage to wangle it, I joined them. I squeezed my few belongings in. On one side of me there was John, and Percy Barr was on the other. And so I was back with the two friends from my own battalion, the men who'd gone into battle with me.

So the last phase of our captivity, spreading from April 1944 to September of the following year, began with quite an improvement in the general conditions. The atap hut provided reasonable quarters, since it had floorboards and windows at intervals. We had a few amenities. Somehow we managed to collect some books and start a camp library. Concert parties were organized and we even built

145

a makeshift theatre which was known as Coconut Grove. There was a repair shop where our old rags could receive even more patching.

The garden produce, in the shape of green vegetables and tapioca root, made the unvarying and unbearable rice a bit more palatable. We were organized into parties for light work during the day and this used to take us outside the actual jail area. There were two main tasks, gardening and wood gathering.

The areas we went to were the same as those we'd worked in the old days when we were in what had been known as the Garden and Wood Area. Apart from the state of our health preventing us from doing any exacting work, the general tendency on the part of the Japs was to improve their treatment of us, and they were even coming round to the idea that officer prisoners-of-war should not be made to work. Remembering the bitter disputes over this in the past it was indeed a change.

The troops inside the jail did have two major work commitments, and one of these was of particular interest and encouragement to all of us. With a few officers from the administrative area to supervise them they were taken by truck into Singapore each day. The work was called construction, but it included the digging of deep foxholes for the Jap army against the possible invasion of Malaya. Their other large-scale task was the making of a large airfield on Changi Maidan. This was the open area where our battalion had been put under canvas shortly after the battle.

Our own wood-gathering parties were less serious; in fact they bordered on farce. We had an old lorry chassis and this was pulled by some twenty-four officers in the traces like carthorses. There were four officers to each of the six traces. The contraption was steered by a wounded officer and the whole party was commanded by a jovial Norfolks major, Charles Wood, who was a farmer in peacetime.

The 'carthorses' had to learn horse language. For example that "Cubby holt" meant haul to the right, and that "Wheest!" meant go to the left. These shouted instructions to the sweating and straining humans in the traces never failed to arouse laughter in us and bewilderment among our Jap escorts.

The jail and its adjoining huts, coolie lines and houses formed an incomplete prisoner-of-war camp area which was surrounded by barbed wire and patrolled by sentries.

Both the gardens and the tree-felling areas were adjoining, but outside the wire. Every party leaving the area had to report in

146

Japanese at the guardroom. Even the customary salutes of "Eyes right" (Kashira migi) and the subsequent "Eyes front" (Narri) had to be given in Japanese.

One of our minor amusements was completely to mystify the Jap sentries. The wood gatherers would often pass through with the order given as "Bullocks, eyes right". Or perhaps "Carthorses, eyes front", or even "Look at him", "You've seen him".

For some reason we could never quite understand there were periods when we were ordered to go into details as to the actual strength of the parties leaving the camp area. These usually consisted of twenty-four men and one leader. So it became necessary to learn the Japanese for twenty-five. It was Ni (two) Ju (ten) Go (five) Mé (men) said quickly as Nijugome.

On one occasion a party of troops was marched by a young N.C.O. past the guardroom. He failed to report the numbers in Japanese and a sentry came running after him, shouting crossly, "Ni-ju-go-me!"

The bewildered N.C.O. answered, "No – I've been detailed."

We found that one daily trip with our makeshift 'dray' was quite enough for our sapped strength. Physically we were betwixt and between. We'd survived the railway slave labour and we were not on the real sick list. On the other hand our capacity for work was very small and we quickly tired. Occasionally I would, even on light labour such as this, be overcome by a dizzy spell or a complete blackout. The only thing then was to sit, or lie down, until it had passed. Fortunately we were not in close contact with the Japs and so if any of us did falter we didn't suffer kicks or blows with a rifle butt, though, under the changing conditions, perhaps violence towards prisoners was forbidden.

We usually managed to be back in camp for lunch and we were allowed to rest in the afternoon. Another welcome innovation was that the weekend was restored. There was no work Saturday afternoons or Sundays.

After a spell of wood-gathering we were switched over to gardening. Here we learnt the way to use a changgol. This is a Malayan tool which I described earlier. It gives a digging effect when the ground is struck with the blade. It's not unlike a strongly constructed hoe with a long blade. We cleared ground for planting.

When this was finished I was transferred to the water-pump and, as quite a bit of physical effort was required, this was scheduled as a mornings only activity. The pump irrigated the garden and to operate it two men stood on a platform and steadied the lever which was worked backwards and forwards between them. The lever had handlebars and the work was not so hard as one would imagine, particularly once the rhythm was established.

I found it quite pleasant to stand in the morning sunshine, stripped to the waist, listening to the steady rhythm of the lever and to hear the precious water spurting out into the irrigation channels which ran along the vegetable beds.

The weeks drifted past, but although the time dragged the establishment of the weekend made a great difference to our spirits. There was usually a concert party or a gramophone recital on Saturday evening in the Coconut Grove open-air theatre.

On Sundays we cleaned ourselves up and generally went to visit the troops in the jail. Sometimes they were permitted to come to the officers' area.

There were about fifty men left from our battalion. Like every other unit in Malaya they'd been split up after the surrender piecemeal all over the place. I think there was a purpose behind this apparently senseless breaking up of units by the Japs. There was an inevitable lowering of morale and a loss of a sense of cohesion – factors which reduced the risk of any revolt or mass attempts at escape. Not that these were ever practical propositions, but the barbaric severity with which any attempts were treated suggests the Japs were nervous.

Somehow or other our battalion C.O., Lieutenant-Colonel Alfred Knights, had managed to take more than half the men to Bukit Timah Working Camp and finally on to Tarsao, where I'd last seen him.

The fifty men who were now at the jail were those who'd been left in Changi area, together with some survivors from F and H Forces.

Now that we were able to exchange experiences it emerged that my working party, H6, had really been unusual in consisting entirely of officers. All the others were mixed, with officers and men from various units, apparently chosen at random.

I heard from Eric Prattley about his battalion. He'd kept most of the men with him until Serangoon Road Camp. Then they dwindled away. The Japs kept varying their demands for labour and didn't, perhaps deliberately, work to any system. One day they'd collect fifty men from various units and send them to Borneo. The next they'd round up five hundred for Siam. It made what command our officers could exercise very difficult indeed. They not only had to reason, so far as reason was possible, with hasty-tempered Japs who were always likely to fly off the handle, but also to maintain some sort of discipline and cheerful spirits among their men, never knowing how many of them would be taken away the next morning.

At the end Eric Prattley was left with only a handful of men, having lost all the others on overseas or up-country parties.

Now that we were back in the Changi Jail area the Japs assured us that there'd be no more parties sent away. I don't think any of us believed them at first. I know I didn't. But gradually, as the weeks and months dragged past, we began to realize they were speaking the truth.

Our Sunday visiting was extended to visits to the hospital, where we still had a number of very sick. And on Sunday evening there was the, to me, fantastic spectacle of what was called 'the goldfish parade'. Every man who could walk took part in this, a steady parade round the camp perimeter, close to the wire. British, Australian, American, Dutch – all took part in what was almost a ritual.

There were several religious services, for we'd quite a number of padres who, between them, were able to offer services to the various sects. I was delighted to renew acquaintance with Padre Duckworth who'd been with us at Serangoon Road. He was the small padre who had once achieved glory as a Cambridge cox.

The services were well attended. I can't tell whether this was out of religious conviction or because the services presented something different in a life which was really terribly monotonous. It's very difficult to write of the monotony. We all suffered from it and had to struggle against its demoralizing effects. It was virtually a disease, rotting away the mind and the spirit. It was progressive and it became more and more difficult to 'snap out of it'. We were all aware of the dangers of running down, but we also knew it was happening and that it always required a bit more effort to check the process. Yet very little can be said of it because monotony is a state of nothing happening.

But to return to the services. I believe that for many men the services did give expression to a faith which had kept them alive and sane on what had been a long march through hell. Without anything to cling to I don't think survival would have been possible. Not for the majority of us. The degradation and the despair and the sheer torment of going on living were such powerful adversaries, and it seemed to me that only an unshakeable faith could beat them in a struggle of endurance.

I don't claim to be a strongly religious person. There's a background. At home as a small child I'd prayed with my mother beside me. There was the rather orthodox teaching of my public school, Blundells, in the West of England. I must have absorbed some faith, more than I suspected, because you don't know what faith you have until it's tested.

To most of us, trudging half-dead along the jungle track, flinging ourselves down with little idea of whether we would ever rise again, prayer became important. It was a thin rope dangling down into the pit.

I think most of us prayed at night and I think we all had moments when something greater than ourselves supported us. Those of us who died found the courage to die and those of us who survived felt that there had been an answer to our reiterated plea: deliver us from evil.

During 3½ years of captivity we received only three postcards to send home from our Japanese captors. On one occasion they had to be written immediately (heaven only knows why they took approximately nine months to get there). A senior Jap N.C.O. arrived whilst we were outside the gaol gathering wood etc., we were called into a semi-circle whilst this man interpreted in broken English, "You very lucky, I bring post cards, you can write home. Now, immediately." Whereupon he distributed the cards and a minute stub of pencil to each man saying, "Only twenty-five words, in BLOCK CAPITALS, you must not say anything bad about Japanese; all cards will be censored." Everyone started thinking and writing. What on earth can one say in twenty-five words? An American officer standing behind the Jap shouted across over one of his shoulders, "Say Reg, how do you spell PRICK . . ."

One card bears repetition: "All Japanese are very nice. Good camp and food. Please tell my comrades in the Army, Navy and especially the Marines. Much love Bert."

# Chapter 9

## TOWARDS THE END OF THE WAR
## 1945

The year spent in the Changi Jail area seemed the longest of my life. I think it was the same for the others. Physically we were more comfortable than we'd been since the earliest days of our captivity. The camp itself was a miracle of improvisation. I doubt if any other in the Far East reached such 'do-it-yourself' heights.

The basic ration of rice was slightly increased, so that we were given more than when we were labouring on the railway. We had, naturally enough, come to loathe the stuff. For health reasons, as well as for relieving the tasteless monotony, we did our best to supply extras. We grew what vegetables we could and we were sometimes able to buy such luxuries as Blachang paste made from dried fish. This was one of the popular lines on sale in the camp canteen.

We had a large number of men suffering from vitamin deficiencies brought about by the limitations of our diet. I was one of them and so the activities of what we called the soup factory – or rather its revolting product – became all too familiar. The working parties which went out into the garden area always cut some of the long grass called lalang. This they delivered to the factory, which was, in appearance, like the laboratory apparatus of a mad scientist.

The lalang was chopped and crushed and generally mangled up until it was reduced to a green slime. This was then fed into a retort which fermented it. I never fully understood the process but my Australian friends thought it was a horrible waste of apparatus because it was right for distilling alcohol. I think it was as well for us that it didn't fall into the hands of the Old Timer and his gang.

Anyway, the concoction produced by the soup factory was very rich in vitamin B and I'm convinced that many lives were saved by it. Its beneficial results, though, did nothing to endear it to the palate. Its taste was so disgusting – like drinking rotten seaweed and green slime scraped out of a sewer – that we were given the mixture under compulsion. All the vitamin deficiency sufferers had to parade, and after forcing down the lalang mixture under supervision their palates were further offended by the issue of a portion of rice polishings. These looked and tasted like sawdust. It was impossible to swallow the necessary spoonful, so the dose was stirred into water and drunk as a paste. Even then it didn't go down easily. The lalang soup always gave me nausea, but I found the best way to tackle it was to close my eyes and swallow as fast as I could. The means were decidedly unpleasant, but the beri-beri and pelagra were combated.

We had another factory which made soap. One cake, about the size of a matchbox, was issued every fortnight. What it contained I've no idea. Its use by skin patients was strictly forbidden, so it certainly didn't comply with the claims of modern soap adverts.

We also made toothpaste, or rather powder, from the fine wood ash carefully sifted from the camp fires. It was really excellent. Gradually the almost universal black teeth faded to grey, and eventually to a yellowish tint.

A most ambitious project was the factory where artificial limbs were made. There was a priority list and every man who'd lost an arm or leg, either in battle or on the railway, was eventually supplied. It was a tremendous undertaking because the list at the start was heartbreakingly long.

On everyday levels we had camp tailors and cobblers. The former had to rely largely upon the green canvas of tent flaps. So the repaired garments, with many patches, began to look like items from a jester's wardrobe. I had a pair of shorts with thirty-six squares of green patching.

Boots and shoes were soled with pieces cut from old rubber tyres. These were nailed, sewn or stuck with latex, which we collected from the local rubber trees.

Finally there was a jeweller's shop where watches, spectacles and such items were repaired. Watches, though, were scarce because most of us had been driven into exchanging them for food long before we reached Changi.

All these services were free, but each application had to be genuine and vouched for by the senior officer in each hut.

It was inevitable there should be a black market as well. I think we all became somewhat involved with rackets, if only by making use of the goods or faculties offered.

The black marketeers had to operate with great caution because their activities were regarded as illegal by our own administration, who were anxious to avoid any 'incidents' which might disrupt the reasonably good relations with the Jap commandant. However, some of the Japs were indirectly involved in the black market themselves. The sentries were often quite willing to buy personal valuables which took their eye. The money could be spent openly in the canteen, or true black market purchases could be made through the wire at night, which meant keeping low until the sentries had gone past.

We had one American sergeant from Chicago whose name was Trackenberg. He was an expert dealer and racketeer in old junk. He used to come around the huts at night. When he reached the hut I was in he'd make a hissing noise. "Psst! Cap'n Boiton – any old stuff to-night?" John had an old watch, a Marks and Spencer job, and we passed this to Trackenberg. He assured us he could do a "swell monkeyed-up jab" on it. Sure enough, he did. He had a mapping pen and, with the aid of a magnifying glass he managed to inscribe "Rolex Oyster" on the watch. He added a coronet beneath the words and managed to find a Jap buyer who believed it was the real thing. The proceeds kept us in food extras for quite a time.

Descending to sheer racketeering, the most lucrative racket involved schoolroom chalk. With a fine saw this was cut into circular discs. With the help of a magnifying glass for accuracy, a line was incised across one side and on the other the inscription M and B 603 was cut. These could be sold to the Japs as sulphonamide pills. These 'tablets' found a ready market among the Jap sentries who apparently found the tablets effective. So much for the element of faith in medicine.

The Japs were very keen on Ronson Lighters, but they were more difficult to fake. One could, however, saw the spikes off the barbed wire and make them into little cylindrical objects to resemble flints and these also could be sold to our poor unsuspecting captors, also for a very good price. Of course none of these things were genuine and never worked, but no Jap would ever report such illicit dealings or take any official action.

In the racketeering community we even had moneylenders. They were prepared to cash cheques – at inflationary rates. So far as I know all these were honoured after the war. But I had a very different experience with a cheque. One of the officers in my own regiment, Tom Eaton, had just sold his watch and was 'in funds'. I asked if he would cash a cheque and he agreed, quoting me an exchange rate which was at par, and very generous indeed compared with the current quotation of the Moneylenders Union. The cash was a godsend at this particular time because we were down to bare rations. We were able to buy tap root, sweet potatoes and the strong, dried fish paste. At the end of the war this officer proved a real benefactor; he tore up the cheque.

The craving for a more varied diet, within the constraints of what very modest luxuries were available, was so great that it became a tremendous temptation to sell the last of one's personal possessions. Mine went. And finally, towards the end of the war, though I didn't realize how near we were to deliverance, I consulted the Old Timer about a back tooth of mine which had a gold crown. He persuaded a fellow Digger, who was a dentist, to remove the gold as an 'under the counter' favour. This was done, painlessly, with a pair of pliers.

Bert sold the small piece of gold for two hundred Jap Malay dollars. He deducted ten per cent, so we received one hundred and eighty. It was far from being a small fortune. We called this Jap currency banana money. Inflation was rife and my sacrifice purchased us ten pounds of tapioca root and sweet potatoes. However, it augmented the diet of our little combine for about a week.

It was not really worth it. The tooth gave me trouble ever after and eventually had to be pulled out. And the war was over within a few weeks.

But to go back. Apart from the constant struggle to do something about the monotonous food there was the inner fight against boredom. Sometimes I found I missed the hustle and bustle of being moved from one camp to another, such as I'd known in the past. I'd always tended to feel fed up then, wishing we could be left in peace somewhere. But during this long period in the Changi jail area I often wished for some real change.

One result of living on top of each other and with so little to do was that personal relationships so easily became frayed. Just as, physically, our bodies were rather worn out, so were our mental powers. If one felt bad-tempered or unusually depressed it became harder and harder to snap out of it. And we were much too cramped in our quarters.

Perhaps it was surprising that we got along as well as we did. Even among such close friends as John and myself, quite trivial incidents could completely poison things for a few days. The most innocent things could be misunderstood and become distorted. On one occasion John gave me an old pair of shoe trees which he'd found somewhere or other. It was a gift. I put them up for sale in the camp shop without consulting him. My intention was to put the proceeds in the kitty for food extras. John was very cross about this and the friction the incident caused lasted nearly a week.

I'd always been on good terms with Percy Barr, but his early morning habit of whistling popular tunes through his teeth nearly made me lose all control and scream at him to shut up. He made matters worse by combing his damp hair over my bunk and giving me a shower in miniature. I'm sure he never realized how jarring this was because I never mentioned it to him.

The crowding was so bad that we'd had to alternate our bunks in order to avoid being head to head. So when I slept at night I had John's feet on my right and Percy's on my left.

The tropical nights were stuffy and hot and I felt that I was dying of suffocation. In the end I had a brainwave and cut a square hole in the wall of the hut. I nailed the top with two leather hinges, and then when night came I used to prop the square outwards and sleep with my head sticking out from the side of the hut. It must have presented a very strange appearance to anyone coming along that side of the hut.

It was generally believed that we were all suffering from T.B. and I think my fresh air device probably helped me to fight it off. How many of us really were affected I don't know. I believe that after we were released Percy had to have a number of check-ups and several X-rays before he was finally cleared.

We did what we could to break up the boredom. There was a library of much be-thumbed books. We had a gramophone record department which toured the camp areas at weekends giving recitals.

This business of keeping ourselves interested was taken quite seriously by our own administration in the camp area. We had an official concert party and its members were excused most of the routine duties so that they could concentrate on entertaining us. They worked hard and did a very good job, some of their productions reaching almost professional standards. They had a large theatre in one of the jail courtyards and amassed a quantity of props and costumes.

Being excused duty they were, of course, accused by some of being 'column dodgers' who had never been up-country. Good-naturedly, they were accused of being layabouts. The Diggers referred to them, very unkindly, as 'bludgers'. This was their amusing slang word for a man living on the immoral earnings of a woman.

Nevertheless, the official concert party really pulled its weight and put on an impressive number of shows. Seats were allocated to the various sub-area inhabitants. Most areas had their own little theatre, and the officers had what was known as Coconut Grove.

The little theatres had a small stage and only odd bits of scenery and props. Several hours before the show was due to start canvas stools and chairs would be arranged. The rest of the audience had to stand at the back. Sometimes the show would be rained off. The tropical storms were usually of deluge proportions and so the only thing to do was to rush for cover.

However, Singapore weather was generally kind, because most of the heavy rainfall happened during the afternoon, leaving the evenings and nights fairly dry. It was very pleasant sitting out in the open air watching a play at night with all the stars clearly defined in the tropical sky above.

Remembering my earlier venture into 'show business' I felt that I'd like to stage a come-back. I started to write a gangster play which I called *Speakeasy*. It was a task which took up a lot of my time, which was no doubt a very good thing. When it was finished I took the script along to the official concert party. They were the obvious choice because they had all the stars and the best resources. Most of them were, or claimed to be, ex-theatre people, though the only one I've heard of since is Syd Piddington. Ronnie Searle (latterly of St Trinians fame) did the decor on the set, and all the camp posters. It was billed as "Burton's Folly Burlesque" or an "American's Impression of an Englishman's Idea of an American Gangster Play". Actually it was probably the best show ever put on in Changi and played to packed enthusiastic houses every night. The pistols and Tommy guns were made of wood, but were so real they had to be inspected and passed as dummies by the Jap Commandant (Takahashi). The Japs enjoyed the show as much as we did and the front row of the stalls was booked for them every night.

Anyway, they were the experts and I hopefully took my play along. My friends were with me and we sat around while they read and discussed it. Their verdict was a great disappointment to me.

They turned it down as unsuitable. So, very crestfallen, I went away.

I was really quite depressed over this. In our 'goldfish bowl' condition any disappointment became something quite big. There wasn't the resilience to help one snap out of it. So it was not unusual for these spiritual doldrums to last many days.

I put the rejected play aside.

American flyers were being brought into our prison camp, a few at a time. After a period of 'solitary' in the jail itself they were allowed to join us, and very welcome they were as they could bring us encouraging news of the allied build-up of strength and the waning power of the Japs. Some of the flyers had been shot down while flying Liberators over Burma, others had been in transport aircraft flying over 'the hump' between India and China, and there were a few fighter pilots shot down along the China coast. These last, of course, were from aircraft-carriers. Through my old pal, the American naval officer Dennis Roland, I was brought rather into this group.

One evening I was sitting in their hut and I'd told them about the play. They commiserated and then one of them suggested that we should form our own acting society. Why not put the play on ourselves? The others received the suggestion with enthusiasm. It was agreed.

I read the script to them. They liked it, but they'd some suggestions. My English had to be translated into American. And a few American jokes should be added. It was all wonderful fun. What had started as an Englishman's impression of an American gangster play became an American idea of an Englishman's impression of an American gangster play. The difference was quite something. Very strange lines appeared in the script such as: "Beat it youse bubs, here comes the cops!"

Every spare moment was devoted to *Speakeasy* and I was rescued from a mental atrophy which had really become quite serious.

My first thought was that I would play one of the leading roles, but when we started rehearsals I quickly found that I couldn't get the accent. The Americans were naturals. My place as the big-shot gangster was taken by Lloyd Jensen from San Francisco, and he looked like a mixture of Humphrey Bogart and Edward G. Robinson. His trigger man, Don Smith, came from Cleveland, Ohio, and was not unlike James Cagney. My friend Dennis Roland gave the performance of a lifetime as a dumb hoodlum.

Stepping down didn't mean that I was out of things. I had to attend every rehearsal as author, but in addition I was assistant producer. I assured the American cast that if a man wanted a quiet life with very little to do, the last thing he should let himself in for was the job of assistant producer. Every conceivable job seemed to be passed to me. I told Lloyd Jensen that he'd taken on something really cushy. What was the lead compared to doing everything in the way of odd jobs?

It was all tremendous fun, but more tremendous still was its reception on the first night. Many of our audiences assured us it was the funniest and finest performance ever put on in Changi. All told we put on six performances – three nights in the officers' area and three inside the jail. While we didn't get a chance of acting on the big stage of the official concert party, some of their members came along to our shows in order to lend a hand. The decor for the set was the work of Ronnie Searle and a Flight-Sergeant Bill Williams was our pianist; we reckoned him one of the finest we'd ever heard.

We had to be cautious with our concerts. Occasionally some of the Japs joined the audience and whenever this happened we had to warn the actors because sometimes they'd 'gag' and bring in some reference to the news.

There was a risky slip-up one night, during a revival of my own French sketch. Lew Martin was taking the part of Papa Dupont and he came on stage reading a newspaper and saying: "What is dis? Germany she surrender – Japan she fight the world alone!" There was a Nip in the audience, right at the back. Lew hadn't spotted him and evidently hadn't received the proper warning. We all held our breaths, but fortunately nothing happened. Some of the Jap privates were very dull mentally and I suspect this one didn't realize that "Japan" was "Nippon" or know what the word "Germany" meant.

The Jap behaviour towards the theatrical ventures was quite unpredictable. Sometimes rehearsals were ignored, at others they'd come along and see what was happening. One day when we were in the middle of a "Speakeasy" rehearsal Jap guards descended on us, stopped us and demanded that we should hand over the wooden tommy-gun which was one of the props. It looked quite bad at first and I was afraid I might be hauled away for questioning and third degree at the hands of the dreaded Kempei-Tai. I began to sweat a bit. I kept saying, "Dummy gun. No fire-ka. Okega!" The Japs carefully inspected the 'weapon' and after what seemed an interminable time they returned it and marched away.

Fortunately, even in their surprise visits, the Japs didn't uncover the source of our news. A band of wireless enthusiasts had managed to rig up a secret set. I believe the officers concerned were R.A.F., but I never knew for sure. It was whispered that the set was hidden in a wall of a hut and operated by using a screwdriver and turning one particular screw-head among the many which were in a wooden beam.

The greatest care was exercised in passing on the news. This grapevine was generally known as 'the pipe'. Certain officers were detailed to go to a rendezvous which was kept secret from the rank and file. Here they were given a résumé of the latest news, which had to be memorized. Memorizing had become a definite order, because, on one occasion, the entire system was endangered by one officer who took notes and was actually reading these to the men in his hut when a Jap sentry walked in, making a surprise check. It was touch and go for a few minutes. One of the men managed to keep the Jap occupied with an exchange of courtesies such as "Oh-hi-yo-go-zi-mus" which was the equivalent of good-morning. While this was in progress the officer had an opportunity to turn his back on the sentry and eat the incriminating piece of paper. This incident produced a spate of 'funny' stories, one of which was that the news we received was so unbelievable that even the chaps dishing it out couldn't swallow it. This, of course, was quite an amusing exaggeration, because we were in receipt of real news and everyone realized this.

Apart from this scare the elaborate system appeared to go un-detected. The one man using the earphones remembered the news and passed it on to a very select team who were, in turn, responsible for relaying it to one representative from each of the lines. Finally it was passed from this representative to a chosen man in each small group for circulation among the rest.

In our hut our 'newscaster' was an officer in my own regiment. His name was Stanley Page and because of his important unofficial job he was nicknamed 'Pipe'. Every lunchtime he would circulate among us whispering the news while others kept a sharp lookout for the Japs.

Sometimes there was very little news indeed. There was a period when day after day Pipe reported in a whisper that the Fourteenth Army had reached the fourteenth milestone on the Tiddim Road in Burma. At last John became impatient. "Come on, Pipe, they were there three weeks ago."

Pipe had a good answer ready. "I can't help it. I'm not commanding the Fourteenth Army."

I said, "If those chaps don't hurry up we'll all be doing life in the ruddy jail.' Pipe grinned. "What are you worrying about, Reggie? This is a jolly good place. Better than Siam. Besides, there's a war on. If you got out you might get killed or something."

As we neared the end of the war it became increasingly obvious that the Japanese war effort was faltering. In another flagrant breach of the Geneva Convention and International Law they started trying to coerce prisoners to help them in their engineering and munitions factories. Each prisoner was issued with a printed pro-forma in English, asking us to state our civilian occupations and qualifications, if any. It was most amusing to note the varied and nonsensical replies they received, to quote but a few – "Cocktail Shakers", "Gigolo", "Dilettantes", "Ballet Dancers", "Bludgers" (Australian slang for layabouts) etc., etc. Everyone was issued with a card which had to be completed giving his precise civilian occupation and an account of the specific duties entailed. It was, of course, against the Geneva Convention to help the enemy to prosecute the war against our people in any way, and we were advised to obey their order to complete the form but to make it out so that it would be of no use to them whatsoever. A few of the replies bear repetition for their ingeniously nonsensical content as follows:

| Occupation | Details |
| --- | --- |
| Dilettante | A lover of fine arts |
| Bar Steward | Cocktail Shaking |
| Gigolo | Professional Ball Room Dancer |
| Male Manneqin | Displaying Contraceptives |
| Pimp | Organizing Call Girls |
| Bumper-upper | Working Mattresses for Tired Prostitutes |
| Bar Fly | Sampling Alcoholic Beverages |
| Bookie's Runner | Placing Bets on Horses |
| Card Sharp | Poker Playing |
| Regular Army Officer | No Ability to do Anything in Particular |
| Manure Man | Dung Heaving |
| Lavatory Attendant | Supervising Public Conveniences |

One would never know what their reaction was to all this; as with most jokes played on these inscrutable orientals, either they did not or would not admit seeing the joke in order to save loss of face. In the end I think people were just drafted to Japan in working parties which had no bearing on the nature of the occupation to be filled.

I was surprised it didn't result in an incident, but apparently it passed off without one, hopefully due to the fact they didn't understand what the occupation meant and most likely they had no sense of humour and couldn't (thankfully) see the jokes. Anyway, the whole matter was forgotten and fortunately no one was selected.

At one point there was a strong rumour that all the working parties in the Changi Gardens were going to be made to cultivate castor oil plants to provide lubricants for the Japanese war machine. I am convinced that as a result of the brilliant American naval victory at Midway the Japs came to realize that they had lost the war.

Generally the news that reached us was cheering, although there were times when the Allies seemed to be making very little progress and we began to feel that there was still a long way to go. We were all confident, though, that we were going to win the war, which certainly hadn't seemed a safe bet at the beginning of our captivity. We were also apprehensive. With things going badly for the Japs what was likely to happen to us before we could be released? Would we be packed off to the hellish railway in a desperate attempt to repair the damage done by frequent bombing raids? Or would the Japs turn on us in a final savagery and massacre us all?

There was a rumour, logical enough, that if an Allied invasion of Malaya took place, the Japs would use us as front-line coolies so that we'd be caught between two fires. The rumour was partly justified because after the war one of the papers which came to light was an order prepared by the Japanese High Command to the effect that we should be used to prepare fortifications for a last-ditch stand. And no doubt we would have perished. Fortunately it didn't come to this, but there was a start on the scheme. Our fittest labour party, known as P Party, was actually used for constructing deep dugouts and strongpoints in certain strategic positions.

Sometimes when there was sensationally good news it was very difficult to hide our excitement. One such occasion was when we had news of Nazi Germany's capitulation.

It is hard to say just how much risk was involved in receiving and circulating the news. There was always the threat of discovery and an investigation by the ruthless Kempei-Tai. But nothing happened and I sometimes wondered whether Takahashi, who, taken all round, was the best Jap officer and certainly the best Camp Commandant we ever met, was turning a blind eye.

Indeed at his trial he maintained he knew there was a secret wireless set and that he'd taken no action. He also vowed that he would certainly never have called in the Kempei-Tai. He said he recognized that in the end Japan would lose the war. Quite a number of his ex-prisoners spoke on his behalf and he was subsequently released.

His motives for such restrained behaviour are a matter for guess-work. Someone suggested: "Leaving the wireless set alone was the only way the poor little bastard could find out what was really happening."

There was suddenly more tangible evidence of the war's progress than the news which came along the pipe. One bright November morning (appropriately, perhaps, the 5th) I was working on the pump in the gardens. I happened to look up in the sky and I immediately stopped work in mingled astonishment and jubilation. High up, flying in formation, there were bombers. They looked like little silver anchors. Jap fighters were climbing, making vapour trails, and there were white puffs from ack-ack shells and the noise of cannon-fire high above us.

We had no air-raid warning system. We learnt afterwards this attack was a complete surprise. The Japs never imagined the Allies could produce a long-distance bomber capable of taking off from Ceylon, raiding Singapore and returning to base. These were, in fact, American B 29s, Superfortresses. They flew on majestically and we could soon hear the heavy explosions as they bombed the naval base at Seletar, not far along the coast from Changi.

We were all cheering, almost delirious with excitement. The Jap guards panicked. They practically ran amok, boxing our ears, slapping our faces and shrieking orders that we were to return to our huts. It took quite a time to restore order.

Air-raid precautions were put into operation by our own camp H.Q. after this raid. Sirens sounded and orders were given for us to return to our huts. Those outside on working parties were to take cover. There were many daylight raids. We always went obediently to our huts and then stood outside and waved to the Superforts passing high overhead.

In an allied air raid over Singapore a Jap fighter, a Zero, was shot down and crash-landed outside Changi Gaol near the main road which ran past the gaol and into Singapore. This crashed fighter, with

162

the dead pilot still in it, was left for a long time for all to see and nothing was done about burying the pilot or salvaging the 'plane. As a result numerous working parties would help themselves to pieces of metal from the wings and fuselage. The aluminium was naturally of a thin gauge and could be prised off between the rivets, in strips. The metal could be concealed on the prisoner's person by wrapping it around the body and buttoning up the shirt. A roaring trade was carried out by the camp workshops making aluminium mess tins, mugs, billy cans, identity discs etc., all thanks to the Imperial Japanese Air Force.

We anticipated that the war would finish in victory for the Allies, but we knew that, for all their faults, the Japs were tough fighters and not likely to give up. So the date for the war's end was something beyond the range of guesswork. I think most of us, so weary now of the long captivity, found it too depressing to calculate how much longer it would last. I believe, too, that most of us had become accustomed, for survival's sake, to living each day for itself that it was hard for the mind to visualize any future.

During the last few months of captivity the news from the secret radio cheered us all up enormously. We learnt that Germany had surrendered and the Americans had taken Okinawa and Iwojima, and were on the threshold to Japan. Rumours were rife as to what our eventual fate would be. Many thought the Japs would massacre us or use us as front line coolies in the event of Malaya being invaded by the Allies. Some thought that in the end we should break out *en masse* as several thousand P.O.W.s could overcome a hundred guards and then escape into the jungles on the mainland.

At this time the Senior Allied Officer (they rotated on a fixed time scale) was Colonel Galleghan, an Australian Officer who had fought gallantly at the battle of Gemas on the mainland. He was known affectionately to everyone as 'Black Jack'. The stories about him were many. He had the uncanny knack of being able to stand up to the Japs without causing a lot of grief and aggro to all and sundry! One particular instance is typical of him: a runner from Camp H.Q. came up to him and said an N.C.O. called Hashimoto wanted to see him. He replied, "If Hashi-bloody-moto wants to see me, he knows where I am"! Whereupon the Australian Staff Officer said, "I can't tell him that, Sir, what shall I say?" B.J. replied, "Well just tell him you can't find me"!

We knew our old friend Bert Saville had known B.J. very well back in Sydney. One day we were discussing what would eventually happen to us. I said that B.J. was considering appointing his old friend Bert as the Officer in Charge of the Escape Committee (actually, as far as I know, none really existed). He would have to co-ordinate all escapes with particular reference to making out forged papers, passes etc. Whereupon old Bert said extremely vehemently, "I am not going to do it. If they took the wire down I wouldn't walk out of here. There is a war going on out there and one could get killed. I'm staying put. Better the devil you know, and anyway, I can't speak their blasted language or even write it!" After this outburst we decided the joke had gone far enough!

The end came so suddenly that we couldn't believe it. One night, just after lights out, there was a scuffling in our hut. I sat up and saw the dim figure of a visitor who was at the bunk of the senior officer of the hut.

I knew at once that there was something urgent and I strained my ears.

All I heard was the senior officer's incredulous "My God! No, it can't be! Are you sure?"

Our visitor departed and the news he'd brought was whispered down the hut. Japan had surrendered. Two atom bombs had been dropped on Hiroshima and Nagasaki. Both cities had been destroyed.

This was followed by the impossible injunction that we were to "Shut up and go to sleep".

Atom bombs? We'd never heard of them. A bomb that could completely destroy a large city? New weapons were invented during wars and no doubt there were much bigger bombs than any we'd known. But these . . .

John and I discussed it in whispers. I felt sure that there was a mistake somewhere. News coming along the pipe passed through so many different people that it wasn't altogether surprising that a message had got mixed up. Against this, so far as we could tell, the news over the past year had been extremely accurate. There was a secret radio working in Changi area, but no one knew where it was or who operated it, for obvious reasons. News, as I have said, was given out in whispers by a hut representative who got it from someone, who got it from someone else etc. etc., and tended to get exaggerated in the process. One night towards the end of the war, long after lights out, a chap from another hut ran the gauntlet of the sentries and, waking the hut commander, carried out a frenzied whispered conversation. In the end I distinctly heard the hut commander say, "You've woken me up to give me this cock and bull story and endangered everyone's lives in the middle of the night. Get the hell out of here." The next morning I asked him what it was all about. He said, "Some bloody fool said we'd dropped an atom bomb in Japan. I've never heard such bloody nonsense in all my life."

We looked anxiously around for confirmation the next morning, but our Jap guards were going about their patrols with the same ugly, impassive faces. But the grapevine news persisted and as the week passed our Japs started to move out. During this period there'd been no further Superfortress raids. So it all seemed true.

Then word was passed round that our guards were being taken away and would be replaced by the dreaded Kempei-Tai. We viewed their arrival with grave misgivings. They arrived sitting in the backs of lorries, rigidly at attention and seeming to stare into space. They were wearing their black steel helmets and had their bayonets fixed. On each arm was the white and red band which was their insignia, and the sight of these armbands brought back many an apprehensive memory.

It was an indication of how different things were, though, that we prisoners could stand around and watch their arrival. We were not pushed and slapped back into line.

The newcomers ignored us as far as it was possible to do so. They took over sentry duties and, instead of rounding us up, they rounded up the old guards and marched them off to some concentration area in accordance with the surrender terms.

In fairness I must record that the behaviour of the Kempei-Tai was extremely correct. Their training and discipline were as superb as their old treatment of suspects was atrocious. It is certain that their presence on guard in the Changi area prevented any attack by demoralized Jap troops on the helpless prisoners-of-war.

We had strict orders that we were not to speak to Kempei-Tai men and that all dealings were to be through our camp H.Q. It was not surprising there was a hundred per cent obedience.

Then, one morning, we saw a group of civilians in white linen suits. They were walking round the officers' area with Takahashi, who still retained his position as Camp Commandant. Word quickly spread that the civilians were neutrals, Swiss actually, who'd come from Singapore and were going to take over control of the camp. We began to crowd round them and Takahashi was actually caught up and jostled a bit. There was still a fantastically unreal situation because the Japs had made no announcement that the war had ended and we couldn't reveal that we knew without admitting that we possessed a secret wireless set, an unthinkable confession with the Kempei-Tai around.

However, this comic-opera situation didn't last much longer. The Swiss had barely taken over the administration when there was, to us, the most exciting moment of our liberation. Parachute troops were dropped in the Garden area. There was terrific cheering and jubilation as they moved among us.

Their officer was a very strongly-built man named Wishart. We offered him a meal of the very best food we could manage, our choicest sweet potatoes, tap roots and the dried fish paste. He looked at the fare without enthusiasm and declined with thanks. He said, "If I eat all that oriental hogswash I'll be ill for the rest of my life!"

He was genuinely shaken when we assured him this was the best we ever had. He said, "Well, if this is the best, God help you. I'd hate to see the worst."

Our food was not the only strange sight to the paratroops. As a last gesture our original Jap guards had issued the camp with what must have been their surplus stores – piles of Japanese cotton and silk underwear. All the garments were too small, even for our emaciated men. But the issue was solemnly made and those men who possibly could were going around in cotton singlets that finished at the navel, and wearing skin-tight, multi-coloured striped underpants. The labels aroused great merriment. Some were very boldly marked 'Superior Quality'. Best of all there were some labelled 'Pure Silk and Emotion'.

The brawny paratroop officer took over from the Swiss civilians and Takahashi. The Kempei-Tai seemed to melt into thin air. And we were at last able to throw away the old rags which had received such hard treatment. We were issued with green uniforms. We received proper food, but we were warned not to eat too much at first and to take it slowly. Instead of the revolting lalang soup we had vitamin pills.

There was soon another change in the camp administration. The paratroops left us and we came under military officials of R.A.P.W.I. (Repatriation of Allied Prisoners of War Internees). No doubt they had their problems, but as time dragged on we maintained the letters should have really stood for Retain All Prisoners of War Indefinitely.

This last phase of our time in Singapore seemed such a muddle, with so many things happening that our minds, which had suffered three and half years of doldrums, couldn't grasp what was going on. Our general feeling was of bewilderment. Everything seemed unreal and as we were given more and more freedom we found great difficulty in readjusting ourselves. No doubt our minds as well as our bodies had suffered and we were neither bright nor alert mentally. A small example was typical. I was free to write home and I tried to write a long letter to my mother. I knew she'd be anxious for all the news of me that she could get. The task proved impossible. I made no end of attempts and tore each one up with an increasing feeling of helplessness. In the end I sent just a few lines to assure her that I was well and would be coming home soon.

Our particular division, the 18th, had been the last to reach Malaya, so it wasn't unreasonable that we should be at the end of the queue. Of course, the Americans and others made their own arrangements for getting their people home. And so there was a succession of farewell parties and our numbers were steadily reduced. The Americans, the Australians, the Indian Army officers, even the Italians, departed.

There was a feeling of luxury, though, in being able to move about the Changi area without bumping into throngs of other prisoners. We were receiving proper medical attention, we were having food which was more natural to us, we were getting letters from home. We were allowed to go out and into Singapore where it was a joyful but almost unreal experience to walk around the streets, to go into shops, to drop in at the officers' club.

There was one very eventful evening just before our Australian friends left us. We went with them and some nurses to a dance at the officers' club. It was a strangely mixed crowd. There were military and civilian ex-prisoners who were sufficiently fit to get out and about, and there were the new arrivals, both military and civilian.

I felt very self-conscious trying to dance again and I apologized to one girl, saying, "I can't dance really. I haven't tried for over four years." She was very charming and said, "You're better than most of the men on the floor at this moment." I looked around and realized I was the only ex-prisoner-of-war who was dancing.

There was one amusing incident during our last few days. The R.A.P.W.I. administration sent a working party of ex-PoWs to the docks, very much as the Japs had done. The men concerned were fit, and no doubt the idea was to keep them occupied. Their job consisted in helping to bring ashore the kit of the incoming troops.

At last it was our turn to leave Singapore. Trucks arrived for us one morning and we drove out of Changi on the way to the docks and the troopship *Sobieski*. As we drove along the familiar roads we passed columns of Japanese troops. They were marching into captivity. I think we can be pardoned for jeering at them. After all, they were not going to suffer at our hands as we had suffered at theirs.

# EPILOGUE

We are always told that time is a healer. It is true that time has brought about a mental and physical recovery, and from this distance I can look back and present a more objective picture of the years of captivity. I have my carefully hidden diary and some notes, but my memory is, I think, remarkably clear.

I have tried to give a fair picture of the Japanese, but time has not healed my bitterness towards them. Perhaps I remember too much too vividly.

In 1958 I was on a posting to the Canadian Army and was sitting in the lobby of a large Ottawa hotel when the members of a Japanese Trade Delegation arrived and checked in at the reception desk. Their manners were polite and inoffensive, but I stiffened in my chair and all the hatred of the captive years came flooding back. I saw not civilians, but the red and white arm-banded and jack-booted Kempei-Tai; not delegates but the inhuman slave-drivers of the Burma railway.

I had a strong but completely crazy impulse to charge across the room shouting, "Kurrah Bugero!" and to box their ears madly. I couldn't stay where I was. I had to walk straight out of the hotel and go round the block a few times.

The Japs gave formal little bows as I passed near to them, and my palms tingled to land them one.

There was another post-war incident. Eventually I returned to Malaya. I was married now and my wife was with me. I took her and some friends to Changi Jail. We stopped at the main gate and I asked to see the warden.

I told him my story and asked permission to take my wife and friends to have a quick look at my old cell in E block. The warden called the superintendent, and the superintendent telephoned the chief superintendent.

Then the superintendent said to me, "I'm sorry, sir. Now we have the emergency in Malaya the jail's being used to house Communist bandits. It's against security regulations for you to have a look round."

I felt a bit crestfallen. I said, "Last time I was here I was inside longing to get out. Now I'm outside wanting to get in. You just can't have everything in life, can you?"

Now, in the year 2002, I feel I must end this new edition by recounting a very poignant episode, a positive note on which to end this account of Japanese captivity.

I had been posted back to Malaya on graduating from the Staff College, to the position of Brigade Major of 99 Gurkha Infantry Brigade. We were engaged in jungle operations against our old allies the Chinese guerrillas. They had started an uprising against the Malayan government and this was known in the 1950s as the Malayan Emergency.

We were based in Taiping-Perak, central Malaya, and it was there that I met a very charismatic character, Father Malone, our Roman Catholic Army Chaplain. We had many discussions about religion and developed a great rapport. I argued for the Protestant belief and he for the Catholic. He was most interested to hear of the men's behaviour in extreme adversity and of how, when all else failed, we came to rely on the power of prayer for help and comfort, and what a sustaining influence it provided.

I told him how much I hated the Japanese for all they had done to us and that I could never forget nor forgive them. I will always remember his reply for as long as I live. He said, "It is your solemn duty to God to expel such thoughts from your mind. You *must* forgive them in accordance with the teachings of our Lord Jesus. The concept of love and forgiveness is the very basis of our religion and the foundation of our Christian civilization."

# INDEX